Beginning Farming

Also by Lowell Christensen

Coping with Texas and Other Staggering Feets

and a few rough chapters outlines for

Intermediate Farming - Working with Clods

1. *Ostriches - As stupid as turkeys, but bigger.*
2. *Hawaii Pineapple Farms - A tax deductible report.*

Beginning Farming

and What Makes a Sheep Tick

by

Lowell T. Christensen

Piñon Press
Los Alamos, NM

Beginning Farming and What Makes a Sheep Tick

Printed in the United States of America.

Publisher's Cataloging in Publication
(prepared by Quality Books, Inc.)

Christensen, Lowell, 1954-
Beginning farming and what makes a sheep tick / Lowell Christensen
p. cm.
ISBN 0-9642483-0-1

1. Agriculture--Humor. 2. Farm Life--Humor. I. Title

S521.C57 1994 630.2'017
QBI94-1737

Published in 1994 by Piñon Press
Post Office Box 4785
Los Alamos, NM 87544

Dedication

This book is dedicated to my parents, who taught me how to milk cows, plant oats, hoe weeds, haul hay, shoot rabbits, herd sheep, make cookies, slop hogs, stay out of the cookie dough, irrigate, and other skills that I firmly believe everyone should be forced to learn.

Acknowledgments

Sincere thanks to those who contributed to this book in any way.

Lisa — Wonderful wife and most reliable editor.

Durbin, Peggy, index created by, tender, luminous and finely wrought: 122

Chris Lindberg — Famed photographer, dragon expert, and artist.

Mary Thomas Brown — Beautiful illustrator.

Clothes and Carrots — Farm supply store.

Ted Larson — Rancher and former owner of a frozen pig's head.

Terry Helm — Ph.D. and turkey expert.

Table of Contents

INTRODUCTION

Millions of people drive to their offices every day to sit in meetings trying to stay awake listening to someone speaking in Gregorian chant explaining pie charts, consensus-building-by-edict, and Total Quality Micromanagement (TQM). Everyone takes notes and looks very concerned, but inside they are all thinking, "With all this training I should quit this job and buy a little farm in the country where I could drive a manure spreader."

Do it! Sell your large house and miniature yard, say good-bye to congested traffic and co-workers, read this book, and become a farmer. This book will help you understand all the basic farming skills you will need:

- how to clean a chicken without using soap,
- what makes a sheep tick,
- why seeds sometimes sprout when you want them to,
- how to milk a cow with minimal risk to your skeletal system,
- and how to make a million dollars at the same time.

You will learn many of the realities of farming, such as how the tomatoes you grow in your farm garden will taste so much better than those orange croquet balls from the store, and forget the million dollars.

This book describes the rudiments of farming, which I will occasionally illustrate by relating my personal experiences growing up on the farm. These descriptions will help you envision what it really is like to slop hogs, plow, chase skunks with a stick, fish with heavy equipment, throw eggs, get chased with a stick, bale hay, and do everything else that makes farm life so wonderful. I have tried to strike a balance between being vividly accurate about, for example, things we did to baby magpies and being sensitive to the innocence of city dwellers, who probably have never played with model rockets.

I grew up in Colorado on what you might call a small farm, or as I say among the *haut monde* (snobbish people who like to interject French words), "I grew up on a Colorado ranch." "Farm" brings to one's mind the image of someone in bib overalls watching beetles eat the only corn stalk that the dust storm didn't destroy, whereas "ranch" suggests a place like on *Bonanza* where you jump on your horse and gallop all day long and never come anywhere near your property border.[1]

As you read this text, you will begin to comprehend why farming is a rewarding profession. To begin with, you do not have to watch people turn into groveling leeches around upper managers. The farm organizational chart has only one box. Standing tall, you work your own hours. Then you collapse. You get to eat excellent food. "Steak again? When are we going to have hot dogs?" You get to witness the miracle of nature — seeds sprouting into blades that turn into oats that slowly mature to get pulverized by a hailstorm, which means there will be plenty of unharvested grain to attract pheasants this year.

Because the book deals with farming basics, it has great potential as a classic college textbook, which means that you must buy it for $45.99, or you will not pass Agriculture 101. So buy several dozen now while it's affordable. After you have finished this book, you will understand enough about farming to drive to a remote spot, purchase some land, build a farm house and some farm buildings, purchase some dangerous machinery, plant seeds, raise some animals, and sit back in your porch

---

[1] Because if you gallop your horse all day like they did on *Bonanza*, it will be dead.

swing with a grass stalk in your teeth and think to yourself, "Why the heck do people chew on these things?"

Discussion Questions:

- What is the world speed record for a baby magpie?
- Are you a rancher if you have a cow?
- Give some examples of ranch dressing.

HISTORY

Let's begin with the fascinating history of farming. The study of history helps us understand the complexities of life by answering such questions as, "What was the year those four men froze to death trying to take a cow to the top of the Matterhorn?" Facts like this are the quest of the dedicated historian. I hope you appreciate that writing accurate history requires hundreds of hours of library research, checking multiple sources, reviewing ancient manuscripts, and standing in line at the photocopy machine.

Farming Among the Neanderthal

As any good archaeologist holding a pottery shard and a few bone fragments in his hand will tell you, prehistoric men were expert hunters. They would run around all day waiting for the dog to flush a covey of pterodactyls so they could hurl their spears into the air and bag a few. Then they would return home with their kill and sit around the campfire telling hunting stories and roasting marshmallows. One Monday morning at the Neanderthal cave meeting, Grock, one of Earth's first environmentalists, said, "Gentlemen, I propose that we cease destroying pterodactyls, which are on the endangered species list, and begin to scrape the dirt with sticks and plant seeds and live off vegetables such as eggplant and Brussels sprouts." A subcommittee, organized to analyze the proposal, offered a counterproposal, "Let's eat Grock." The rest is history.

The First Garden

Adam was the first modern, civilized, Southern-Baptist-approved man. God planted a garden and put Adam there to name all the animals (newt, dingo, brontosaurus, Jersey cow, etc.), and he put Eve there to remind Adam that the name "brontosaurus" is passé. Adam was doing quite well in the Garden of Eden until he made a big, big mistake, and this should be a powerful lesson to the rest of us — if you see a snake in your garden, kill it! God expelled Adam and Eve from the garden into the real world where there were discomforts and plagues such as thorns, germs, neckties, Nintendo music, and public television fund drives.

As Adam's family populated the earth they strove toward the ideal of growing food, namely, if you can get someone else to grow all the food while you take it easy, that's ideal.

Egyptians

The ancient Egyptians built a successful farming and food storage system based on Pharaoh's dream where he saw seven skinny cows eat seven fat cows. Living in hot sandy places will cause dreams like that. I, for one, wonder about that dream. If it had been chickens, I would believe it, but cows? If it had been seven skinny cows eating seven fat ears of corn, that happens a lot. "Hey, how did those @&*!# cows get in the garden?" But cows do not eat cows. I'm sorry. They just don't have the stomachs for it. But if cows ever do become carnivorous, maybe we had better start worshipping them, just as a precaution.

After Pharaoh's dream, the Egyptian farming system gradually changed to having Israelites do all the work while the Egyptians spent their time swatting flies and watching incendiary mothballs fall from heaven. The Israelites finally realized that their standard of living would improve if they moved to the promised land, so Moses told Pharaoh, "Let my people go, or we will fly in below radar and wipe out your entire Air Force."[1] After the Israelites left, the Egyptians built a farm economy based on barely surviving between flooding seasons.

One Egyptian crop that changed the world was papyrus, which they used to invent paper. Papyrus paper was a good source of fiber, but it tasted terrible. Then someone came up with the idea of using paper to doodle on during boring

---

[1] From *The Ten Commandments*, starring Moses as Charlton Heston

meetings. This led to the invention of a written language consisting of a bunch of wiggly lines and cartoons.

For centuries everyone thought that the Egyptian language was just a bunch of wiggly lines and cartoons, but in 1756 the English[2] invaded Egypt and captured the Rosetta Stone that you can see today in the British Museum surrounded by Japanese tourists.[3] The Rosetta Stone has the same message inscribed in three languages: Egyptian, Jive, and Japanese. Scholars translated the writing on the stone and discovered that whoever wrote the message had severe mental problems.

"Farm income should be reported on line 9 of Schedule F. Farm loss due to the flooding Nile river can be deducted using Form 234, Part D if your loss is greater than the least of your adjusted mud hut value and the standard deduction on line 12."

Greeks

The early Greeks developed a nearly ideal farming system in which the slaves made olive oil that brought in enough money so the Greek men had enough spare time to sit around most of the year discussing philosophy, roasting marshmallows, and playing games. One of their favorite games was to dare each other to eat something really gross, such as mutton and rice wrapped in a grape leaf, and then kill the taste with a gob of baklava.

The Greeks also discovered zucchini. We know this because of Greek mythology, which scholars now admit is just an exaggerated account of man trying to understand things like

---

[2] Someone should tell the English that papyrus doesn't make very soft toilet paper.

[3] Japanese tourists surround both the Rosetta Stone <u>and</u> the British Museum.

gardening before we had Victory Garden. Take Hercules and the Hydra for instance.

The Hydra was a monster with several heads, one of which was immortal. Hercules struck off a head, but two new ones grew in its place. He finally destroyed the monster with fire and buried the immortal head under a rock. It is obvious that Hercules had fought with an early zucchini plant.

Greek mythology also answers the age-old question: what are we going to do with all this zucchini? Hercules was on the way to get some golden apples, but he decided to negotiate a trade — he would hold the earth on his shoulders while Atlas went to fetch the apples. Atlas returned feeling quite free and liberated and full of apples, so he told Hercules to hold the earth for the rest of eternity himself. Hercules said, "OK! I will, but I need you to carry it for a second while I get a better grip." The gullible Atlas fell for it and holds the earth to this day.[1]

You do the same thing with zucchini. Walk along the street until you meet someone. Then say, "Would you mind holding this earth-sized bag of zucchini while I tie my Olympic sprinting shoes?"

Romans

Based on my research, which consists of watching *I, Claudius* on Masterpiece Theater, I learned that the Romans lived on poisoned figs and mushrooms. They also had way too much lead in their wine goblets. The only way to survive as a Roman was to drink unleaded wine and stay as far away from Caligula as possible.

---

[1] NASA report www/jpl.nasa.gov/spacephotos/

Roman farmers grew a lot of pasta and raised Roman Meal bread, but perhaps their biggest contribution to agriculture was bologna. This helped solve the age-old problem of what to do with cow lips.

Vikings

The Nordic countries had a short growing season, so rather than farming, the Vikings invented the basic trade principle of Economics 110 — if you are skilled in one thing, and someone else is skilled in something else, it is more economically efficient to specialize and do your own thing. The English were skilled in producing delicious food and beautiful women. The Vikings were highly skilled in sailing to England, plundering villages, and carrying off all the good food and beautiful women. This explains why today's Scandinavian women are beautiful and why the English eat Brussels sprouts.

Medieval Farming

In feudal Europe (located approximately where Euro-Disney is today) the farm system consisted of a bunch of serfs who worked all day in the fields and lived on gruel. They were at the bottom of a caste system,[1] meaning they were expected to bow very low in the mud when the Marquis Geranium du Puer les Count de Manureaux rode by on his way to another feast at the castle. The castle was in the middle of town, and when the English would invade,[2] all the serfs would flee toward the

---

[1] A social order still popular in some corporations today.
[2] Desperately looking for soft toilet paper.

fortification where they would see that the drawbridge was up and all the people inside were laughing at them.

Occasionally a group of serfs realized that the caste system was not fair so they all caught the bubonic plague. The main lesson to be learned from medieval farming is that all of those people are now dead.

Spanish

In 1532, Pizarro conquered the Incas and shipped all their potatoes back to Spain. Ferdinand and Isabella found potatoes to be bland and tasteless so they gave them as a gift to the English along with their daughter, Catherine of Aragon. Henry VIII appreciated the potatoes and even began to look like one, but he eventually divorced Catherine so he could marry Anne Boleyn with whom he was head over heels in love. The National Enquirer had a field day.

Discussion Questions

- Did the Garden of Eden have lima beans?
- Using Greek mythology, explain the reason we have boiled okra.
- Would it have been fun to be a Viking? Explain.

Farming in America

The Pilgrims fled England to escape the dreadful War of the Potatoes. They arrived in the New World and promptly began starving to death. Luckily, some Indians, with degrees from Texas A&M, taught the Pilgrims how to plant corn and pumpkins and shoot turkeys and sit around watching the Detroit Lions play the Dallas Cowboys while the women cooked and served a big feast. The Pilgrims were very grateful to the Indians and promised to let any of their surviving descendants live in Oklahoma.

As the colonists expanded westward, they chopped down trees to clear land for farming, little realizing that their efforts would cause global warming, melt the polar ice caps, and within a few years obliterate all life on the planet. Luckily, in 1783 a volcano in Iceland blew its top and spewed out tons of ash that hid the sun for several months, cooling the planet down again. This was a close call, so Americans began hunting for places to farm where they didn't have to chop all the trees down. This led to the discovery of Kansas in 1826 by the famous American explorers Herbert and Wilma Snodgrass and their twelve children.

Farming in the vast prairie was difficult work. Farmers used oxen to pull the plow, and these were oxen without air conditioning and the optional CD player. It is obvious, in hindsight, that these farmers needed modern tractors. Most of the other farm tasks, such as harvesting the wheat crop, were also very difficult and labor intensive without the aid of machines. Something had to be done, and American inventors rose to the occasion.

In 1835, Walt Whitman invented the cotton gin, which proved to be totally useless for harvesting wheat. This was very upsetting to the Kansas farmers, and there is still a large reward out for that salesman.

Other inventions followed, and soon farmers discovered the key to modern farming. You can increase crop production, minimize labor, eliminate the need for oxen so you can eat them instead,[1] and get hopelessly buried in debt by buying lots of hazardous farm machinery.

Inventors developed new hazardous machines, and farmers discovered new crops as the nation expanded. For example, in the mid-1800s Percy Y. Gibbons discovered artichokes in California, but this important farming news did not get the front page coverage it deserved because of the gold rush.

This was the beginning of the heyday of farming. Settlers began harvesting passenger pigeons and buffalo, distillation devices boosted the farm economy of Arkansas, Ponce de Leon discovered Florida orange juice, Cyrus McCormick patented the grim reaper, Cajuns planted crawfish farms in Louisiana, and everything looked just fabulous for farmers, though they were, as usual, just barely getting by.

To keep farmers humble there were a few farming disasters such as the Dust Bowl caused by poor farming techniques, improper crop rotation, wind, dust, and the NCAA. Still, farming survived, and today it is an important part of our economy in that without it we would all die.

America is now home of the Breadbasket, Amber Waves of Grain, the Fruited Plain, Idaho, and other famous farming features. Each region and climate favors its own unique crops and livestock. For example, grapefruits grow in Florida; Texas raises decorative cattle; pyrogenic green chile is harvested very carefully in New Mexico; wheat grows in the Midwest; and corn and spontaneously generated pigs grow in Iowa. California

---

[1] Oxen are now extinct.

grows nuts and strawberries, and Georgia is famous for kudzu and goober farmers like Jimmy Carter.

Discussion Questions:

- Who won the ball game on that first Thanksgiving?
- Do you make a dry martini with cotton gin?
- Where did oxen come from?
- What exactly is a goober? Would you invite one to a dinner party?

LAND

Before you begin to farm, you must grab some land. The choice of land will influence the success of your farming experience. I would recommend land with good top soil, plenty of available water, and located where Disney plans to build its next theme park.

Buy as many acres as possible. An acre is 160 square rods. This may seem confusing because most rods are cylindrical, but a farm rod is 5.5 yards, and I don't know if this refers to front or back yards. It really doesn't matter.

The price of land will vary from a few cents per acre for a toxic landfill to several million dollars per acre if you land on Boardwalk and Park Place and have passed "Go" often enough to purchase them.

Before purchasing the land, you should examine the soil. You should have professionals evaluate your soil by taking it to your county agent, who will send it to a university with a name that ends with A&M, i.e. Yale A&M. They will study your soil and send you back a report that looks like this.

Soil Evaluation

Inorganic	
Sand	25%
Dust	20%
Clay	10%
Grits	10%
Iron	3%
Potassium	1%
Heavy Metals	5%
Soft Rocks	2%
Classical	4%
Spent rim-fire .22 cartridge	2%

Organic Matter	
Some dried-up worms	4%
Composted grass and weeds	18%
A small bone	1%
Something we couldn't identify	4%
Monosodium glutamate	<1%

You want plenty of organic matter and some basic elements like iron, lead, mercury, platinum, etc. You should think twice about purchasing the property if they find fresh, radioactive timber wolf droppings, but often this is just a laboratory error that you can ignore.

If the soil lacks certain essential nutrients such as niacin, zinc, zirconium, sodium benzoate, etc., add these by burying a dead fish under each corn seed.

Soil is not the only thing you must evaluate. You must decide where your irrigation water will come from. There are several sources.

1) Rain - This is an excellent source of water, especially if you know the right dance steps; however, rain often refuses to come when your seeds are trying to sprout, and it waits until you have cut your hay to dry in the field before coming in torrents.

2) Ditch - This is a great source of water, and it gives you a great place to fish, throw rocks at floating cow pies, kayak, and swim. Owning a ditch means you will have the pleasure of attending ditch-board meetings where you and your friends and neighbors will periodically meet to yell and threaten each other.

3) Wells - These are holes in the ground from which you pump water for your crops. Wells are expensive to operate, and they are poor sources of fish. You will, of course, need a few wells, one for your house and a few to pump water for your cows in the winter when there is no ditch water.

(Kids: Try this at home. Drop a fireplace brick down a well shaft. The echo of the splash sounds really neat.)

You can have a little pump-house built over the well so you will have a roof over your head when you are thawing water pipes in the winter, or you can do what we did and build your actual residence over the well.

You can buy a good submersible pump from Sears and thread pipe sections on to it until the pump is down the shaft far enough to hit fireplace brick. In our case that was only a few feet.[1]

Discussion Questions

- How do you make a cow pie float?
- Which of the following would not be allowed at a ditch board meeting: reservoir level records, headgate drawings, Pepsi, semi-automatic weapons?
- Which should you bury with pumpkin seeds, mahi-mahi or halibut?

---

[1]Our sire, on that occasion, expressed his sentiments with much eloquence.

TOWN

Somewhere within one hundred miles of your farm will be a town that will provide essential shopping and social facilities. This town should have a feed store, a grocery store, a church, a post office, a school, and a service station. The service station is the social hub of the community. You will always find four or five locals who spend their entire lives at the filling station. These locals are given names like Rainbo - the Eight-hour Loaf, the Vegetable, or Jabba-the-Hut. Their niche in life is to sit on a bench at the filling station and drink Coke or chew tobacco. When you enter the filling station to pick up your repaired tractor tire, the locals will greet you with some friendly and intelligent remark such as, "Burp."

Local law enforcement consists of a town sheriff whose job is to go arrest the town thief for any crime committed, which usually consists of breaking into the grocery store and stealing something of minimal value, like the cash register. The sheriff is paid out of revenues accrued from his fining out-of-state people for flagrant traffic violations such as parking more than twelve inches from where the curb would be if there was one.

Your children will attend a school in town. Let me reassure your children: Listen kids, rural schools offer superior teaching environments because the teacher somehow knows everything about you. The teacher will require you to read and memorize college-level literature in fourth grade because, "I know you can do it, and don't pretend you can't or I'll draw and quarter you!" You will not get away with late or shoddy work, mediocrity, theatrics, or laziness like the rest of this country's spoiled youth, especially since you are her nephew.

One day I looked up "draw and quarter" and was relieved to find it described as a less severe threat than I had imagined.

Discussion Questions

- Rank the following professions in order of something you would encourage your child to become: Federal Reserve Chairman, Queen of England, professional baseball player, service station local.
- What is the speed limit through town if you have out-of-state plates?

Town Celebration

Once a year your town should hold a celebration named after your town and a vegetable, something like the Hicksville Pinto Bean Festival. The day should begin with a parade that leads off with a pickup festooned with loudspeakers bellowing out invitations to attend the Bean Barbecue, Bean Games and Pinto Rodeo, Bean Barn Dance, and Bean Fireworks.

Next you will see a float made from a hay trailer decked with cardboard, tin foil, fiberglass angel hair, and various other decoration materials not meant to be exposed to today's rain, including the Pinto Bean Queen and her retinue. The Pinto Bean Queen should be a young, attractive girl who knows how to wave.[1]

Following the Queen's float should be a herd of cowboys on horses or some other hoofed animals followed, appropriately, by B. Arnold Grubber, a man who is driving a tractor, wearing a three-piece suit, and running for county commissioner.

Next will be the Hicksville Big Bean Band consisting of a 1972 pickup carrying Gladys Hicks, accordion; Horace

---

[1]Not like Queen Elizabeth.

McGraw, snare drum; Eunice Hopper, bass clarinet; Clyde Bob "Anthrax" Jones, cello; and Erastus Hicks, vocal.

The rest of the parade should consist of more floats, more cowboys on horses, and a group of go-cart driving Shriners wearing silly hats whose purpose is to show up at a parade and make bean farmers feel extremely dignified.

After the parade you should dash over to the Bean Barbecue for lunch, then on to the Bean Games where you can engage in three-legged races, greased pie catching, and pig eating contests.

The Pinto Rodeo will feature men with comical hats riding horses and sometimes cows. The rodeo begins with cowboys and cowgirls on horseback getting hopelessly confused doing the Virginia Reel while you are out getting a hamburger ($3.95). Next will begin a series of events known in rodeo lingo as "events:"

- Events where animals try to kill you - bronc riding, bull riding.
- Events where you try to get even - calf roping, steer wrestling.
- Events where the audience will be very bored - barrel racing

The evening Bean Barn Dance is where you and your lovely date can dance in a barn. The dance begins with the Grand March where everyone will get dreadfully disoriented to the tune of "The Colonel Bogey March.[1]" Then the "caller" will direct you to perform various square dance maneuvers in which you will become hopelessly confused to the tune of "Fly in the Buttermilk" by Kermit the Frog.

Square Dance Essentials

Promenade	Hold your partner's hands and walk around in a circle while the caller tries to figure some other call that won't result in total chaos.
Do-si-do	Fold your arms and walk toward the object of your do-si-do and pass right by to her right (stage left) and then move past her, back to back, and then move to the head couple spot unless you belong to one of the side couples.

---

[1] From the classic movie, *The Bridge on the River Kwai.*

Swing your corner	Grab the lady at your left by her right arm and swing her around once or twice depending on how fast a swinger you are, how much you are ahead of the music and her weight.
Bow to your partner	Go find your date, wherever she is, and bow to her.
Star right	This involves the four guys joining right hands and walking around in a circle in the center of the square with at least one of the four guys walking backwards.
Alamode left	Take your corner by the right hand, and walk past her and try to remember to let go of her hand (unless the two of you want to slip outside for some fresh air and watch the sun set over the potato field) and grab the next lady by the left hand and so forth until you eventually end up with someone you want to dance with.

The high point of the dance is when someone dashes in and announces that the fireworks have begun.

Pinto Bean Fireworks -This should be self-explanatory.

Discussion questions:

- What festival changes would occur if they suddenly decided to plant onions in Hicksville?
- A cello?
- Do you think that *The Bridge on the River Kwai* was a better movie than the mindless and morose Batman movies?
- Do you think that women weighing over three hundred pounds should be allowed to wear those puffy plaid square dance skirts?
- How about men in severely tight jeans where their belt buckle is hidden by their belly?

HOUSE AND STRUCTURES

The best way to start out living on the farm is to go into debt by buying a farm with an old farmhouse on it. This will give you a roof over your head while you build a new farm house. Build the new house around the old one, and throw the old house out the window.

You must next build a barn, granary, shop, root cellar, chicken coop, pig boudoir, sheep shed, pump house, and, depending on how much money you have left, an outhouse.

If you can afford it, you ought to build another house down the road a ways and give it to the county commissioner. That way you will be sure to have a well-paved road, prompt utility repair, immediate snow removal, and access to a natural gas line.

The farm barn provides shelter and equipment for milking cows and space for hay, salt blocks, tractors, trucks, old cars, sick animals, kayaks, branding equipment, and ropes. Build a big barn, at least six times as big as your house. Use your barn to store equipment, breed cats, deliver lambs, and shoot matches out of your BB gun at the walls. You can also use the barn as a place to butcher pigs and hold dances.[1]

The farm shop should be about as big as the barn. The shop is where you will have your welding machine, chain saws, torches, woodworking equipment, lathe, several tons of wood and scrap metal, several cats, an assortment of nuts and bolts (but not the ones you need immediately), and lots of sharp tools.

I liked the shop because it gave me the opportunity to practice first aid on myself, and I made lots of things: kayaks, wooden guns, spears, a tree house, golf clubs, a pheasant trap (it worked, but the dog got there first), and sparrow whackers.

Farm Decor

Farmers do not have much time or money for lavish landscaping, so most rural homes have the landscaping style, *ambiance du Rover* (let your dog doo your landscaping). A dog, it turns out, is one of nature's natural landscapers. You can help a little by keeping a neatly trimmed lawn in front of the farm house where the dog can tastefully display a cornucopia of rabbit fur, sheep bones, your underwear off the clothesline, various rodent parts, and a substance that will make you very angry and say bad words when you step in it on the way to church. The variety and quantity of farm landscaping is only limited by how many dogs you own.

Humans may attempt to take control of farm landscaping, but it is usually not worth the time and effort. Your wife may decide to plant some daffodil bulbs along the front of the house, but the dog will dig them up and hide them under the pine tree

---

[1]Not on the same day, or your reputation in the community may suffer.

near the dead cat. This should teach you that a farm daffodil bed, if you really want to have one, should be ornamented with an electric barbed wire fence and sharp bamboo shoots.

Many farmers make some attempt to augment the dog's landscaping by parking a totaled '49 Ford pickup on blocks out by the wood pile. This is still perfectly acceptable. An old washing machine on the front porch, however, is acceptable decor only if you are a goober farmer.

Discussion Questions

- Discuss the possible consequences of shooting matches in the barn. (Yell your response to this question!)
- Make complete architectural drawings for a chicken coop. Take no more than three minutes.
- Discuss the environmental impact of a pigpen.
- How do you feel when you are sitting in church listening to a beautiful sermon about loving your neighbor, and the idiot behind you is clipping his fingernails? Explain.

TO HAVE A COW

You need to have some cattle on your farm because it is a nice way to get to know your local veterinarian. You will also have plenty of fresh milk with little clods of stuff floating on top of it. (Do not be alarmed; this is usually just cream.)

The dictionary defines cattle as, "Various animals of the genus Bos," who, you will recall, was an Oklahoma linebacker famous for branding the sides of his head and wearing ear tags. We will confine our discussion of cattle to the species Taurus, a Ford Motor Company word meaning "cow."

There are three types of cows: beef, dairy, and a school principal I once knew.

Beef Cattle

Beef cattle come in a variety of breeds. You must own at least one beef cow to be classified as a rancher.

Black Angus - A breed famous for starting a chain of restaurants.

Hereford - A breed capable of living on sagebrush and cactus, and tasting like it.

Charolais - A French cow famous for red meat, with a subtle bouquet, not too light, quaint but refreshing. I would recommend the charbroiled Chateaubriand; goes well with A&W root beer.

If you arrive at the livestock sale and you can't decide what breed you want to buy, just ask for a few cows named for some place in England. Mosey on over to a group of cowboys and say something like, "I want to buy some of them North Herefordlandshire cows." This is usually effective, but you may be embarrassed to realize, after a few weeks of observing your new herd, that your beef cows are actually milk cows or hogs.

You can experiment with different breeds of cows. Daddy did artificial insemination, and he liked to play invent-a-cow. He would cross-breed the cows just to see what would happen. Once he had a large-boned, tall Holstein milk cow bred with Charolais bull semen from a bull named something like Monsieur la Bull du Mr. Elephant. The resulting calf grew into the largest cow on the face of the earth. It could block several lanes of traffic. Daddy liked having cows like that because he knew that if anyone tried to steal a calf, the cow (mom) would teach the thief the necessity of running forty miles-per-hour in a plowed field and leaping over a six-foot barbed-wire fence.

Discussion Questions

- Where in England did the Charolais originate?
- Shouldn't the government regulate cattle invention?
- How do you choose the best cow to butcher to feed your family?
- How about the one chewing on the tractor spark plug wires?

Dairy Cows

Dairy cattle are bred for milk production and slobbering. We generally kept a couple of fresh milk cows, and it was often my chore to milk them, especially if it was cold outside. Often in January, it was forty below zero outside, and I had to break the milk off in sticks and bring them in to thaw out on the stove.

How to Milk a Cow

You must master this skill if you are ever going to make it on a farm.

You will need a one-legged stool, a strong, clean bucket, a scoop shovel, a filthy bucket, some hobbles, and a clip.

Drive the cow into the barn, and lock its head in the stanchion. To coax the cow to put its head into the stanchion, you will need a bribe. Ground oats work well for experienced cows. Nothing works for a heifer. To get a young cow to stick its head into a stanchion for the first time, requires you and several of your older children armed with sticks, persuasive vocabularies, and possibly a rope.

Once the heifer is in the barn, slowly coax it toward the open stanchion, speaking softly, but carrying a big stick.[1] The heifer will cautiously nose toward the opening, when suddenly a yowling tom cat will pounce onto a female cat hiding under the grain trough. The alarmed heifer will panic, which may require you to drop your stick and run for your life.[2] You may eventually have to rope the heifer and pull its head through the stanchion posts.

Now grab the hobbles and, while trying to avoid being kicked, fasten one clip to the cow's rear left leg and swing the chain around to secure the other leg. The cow may have a stomach disorder, and the tail may be completely disgusting. Here it may be wise to clip the tail to the hobbles to avoid being slapped across the face while milking. Usually the clip works free, however, and you will be slapped across the face with a disgusting tail with a dangerous metal clip attached.

---

[1] A quotation by Teddy Roosevelt about dealing with dairy cows.
[2] The little dog laughed to see such sport.

Clean the cow's milk-producing region to remove anything revolting. Position yourself on the one-legged stool and place the clean bucket between your legs to catch the milk. Now, milk the cow. No amount of written instructions can teach you. This is something that you will just have to learn on the job. At first it seems impossible, and the cow, sensing that you have no idea what you are doing, will step firmly on your toe, but keep trying.

After you have about half a bucket of milk, the cow will step in the bucket. Do not be alarmed; this is normal. Just cuss loudly and try to lift the cow's leg out of the bucket. (Never allow anyone into your barn with a video camera.) The cow will generally assist in removing its hoof from the bucket by kicking it, the hobbles, and possibly you across the barn. Once you have fed the hoof-flavored milk to the cats, rinsed out the bucket, and resumed milking, the retromingent cow will suddenly lift her tail and arch her back. This is your signal to make a split-second decision. Do you grab the filthy bucket, the scoop shovel, or do you just get the heck out of the way?

Soon you will be able to milk a cow in record time, and you will have forearms the size of Popeye's.

Discussion Questions:

- Why do they say “dairy farm” instead of “dairy ranch”?
- Why is it important to know the difference between a cow and a bull?
- What is the difference between a fresh milk cow and a stale one?
- Explain the difference between a beef pie and a cow pie?

Interlude

Picture yourself at the world renown Front-de-Bœuf restaurant in Mud Butte, South Dakota. The lights are low. You and your date have just finished your salads except for the croutons, and your main course has just been placed before you: prime rib (medium rare), baked potatoes with everything (except olives), parsley, some *au jus* and horseradish sauce, and *vegetable du jour* which today is canned peas. There are three things you should not do at this particular moment:

- mash up your canned peas with your fork,
- tell your date what they put in potted meat, or
- stand on the table and loudly read the following section.

Cow Diseases

Blackleg - Gas gangrene in cows. Usually fatal. Also refers to someone who cheats at gambling. Both may be cured by amputation. Prevented by injecting vaccine into the neck of the calf or gambler during branding.

Bloating - Caused when a cow eats too much green alfalfa. Stomach gas production exceeds cow's belching ability. Cow takes on shape and size of Goodyear blimp. Fatal unless you are there and know what to do. Cured by swift action with a long knife and an umbrella.

Brucellosis - A disease caused by the bacillus *Brucella abortus* and resulting in calf abortions. Cured by branding a small B on each cow's neck and selling your herd for dog food. We did this once.

Death by Small Metal Object - This is caused by a cow eating hay or grass with a piece of wire or a nail or something else along for the ride. Once inside the cow it can penetrate one of the stomach linings and find its way to the heart. I helped the vet operate on a cow once to see if he could find anything like that in the cow's stomach. He gave the cow a spinal and cut a hole, and he stuck in his hand and then his arm. He probed the digestive system for foreign objects as well as he could without scuba gear, found nothing, and sewed the cow back together. Sometimes, to avoid barnyard surgery, you must persuade a cow to swallow a cow-belly magnet that will hold onto metal objects to keep them in the stomach.

Lump Jaw - Ordinarily associated with professional baseball players. Caused by a foxtail seed or some other foreign object lodging in the cow's chin tissue and causing a swollen infection. Treatable by barnyard surgery. Not fun to watch.

Bovine Amnesia - Cow suddenly forgets its name and walks around with a stupid look on its face. Hard to diagnose.

Difficult to cure, although some have reported improvements using taxidermy.

Ketosis - The cow will show up to work one day drooling, walking in circles, and chewing on nothing. About the only thing abnormal will be her overpowering fingernail polish remover breath. Keep cow away from sparks or open flame, and hope the problem goes away before there is an impressive detonation.

Blackie the Black Cow

I included this story because it shows that a cow would rather die of natural causes than hang around a packing plant.

Blackie was a black Angus beef cow, but somewhere along the line she inherited milk cow features that were so big they were difficult to grasp. Blackie produced much milk, but her production began to show peculiar aberrations. I discovered one day that Blackie had been drinking her own milk.[1]

Now, what does one do with a cow with this problem? The local ranch supply store had a silly looking little trap door that attached to Blackie's nostrils and came down over her mouth that would allow her to eat and drink water but prevent her weird milk-drinking habit. It didn't work. You would have thought that the other cows' teasing would have deterred her. "Hey, Armor Nose! What's your problem?" Unfortunately, Blackie did not understand anything but, "Moo," so her behavior continued.

Somebody told Daddy that a horse collar slipped on backwards onto the cow's neck would prevent her from reaching the supply, but that failed. Finally Daddy fabricated a medieval-

---

[1] Another futile attempt at perpetual motion.

looking contraption that would keep Blackie essentially looking forward. Houdini-cow somehow managed to figure out a way to continue her alternate lifestyle.

We finally gave up. Daddy trained about four Holstein calves to think that Blackie was “Mom,” and he trained Blackie to accept her new family, and she now had too much competition for her milk. It was a brilliant plan. We turned Blackie out with the beef cows, whereupon she developed a heart condition known as brisket (treatable by moving to sea level) and died.

Years later I would pause at the skeleton. “Alas, poor Blackie. I knew her, Horatio.”[2]

Branding

In the spring you will need to round up the cows on horseback or tractor and separate the calves for branding. By branding I mean branding, earmarking, castrating, vaccinating, and de-horning. Before you start farming, make sure that you can do this interesting work.

You will have to get used to loud bellowing and getting blood all over yourself, and this is from just trying to hold the calf in place in the branding chute. The calf will also bellow and bleed.

Branding involves burning various letters and shapes on the side of your calves so the cow that was somehow locked in the schoolhouse over the weekend can be identified as yours. Critics charge that branding is cruel, and calves should be

---

[2] From Hamlet, played by Mel Gibson who unfortunately gets killed at the end of the movie.

treated more humanely. I say it can't be as bad as a root canal. You don't see calves lying in bed for two days after branding do you?

Earmarking gives you the opportunity to cut identifying notches in the calf's ear while talking to your son about what might happen if he ever wears earrings.

Castrating is taking a surgical tool like one of those displayed in the Tower of London and turning the bull calf into a steer calf. Why is this necessary?

- Which would you rather be in charge of: a field full of docile steers chewing their cuds or a field full of fighting bulls trying to decide which one is *el toro supremo*?
- What would your neighbor want across the flimsy fence from his dairy cows: A field full of docile steers chewing their cuds or a field full of highly excited bulls?
- Do you really want to spend four hours chewing a steak?

Vaccinating protects the calf from Blackleg and other diseases. The shot is administered during branding, when it will hardly be noticed.

De-horning - Using some other Tower of London instruments, you remove the cow's horns. A cow without horns will stop honking at the other cows.

Adopt-a-Cow

Cattle farming is not for everyone so I am pleased to announce that there are alternatives. I am, of course, talking about Adopt-a-Cow, located at Gita-nagari Village in rural Pennsylvania. At Adopt-a-Cow, for $30.00 per month, you can help a cow or ox live a cruelty-free life.[1] You will receive an 8 x 10 photo of your new family member, and adoption certificate, the quarterly newsletter, and other gifts. You will also receive a information about how all humans should be vegetarians.

I like to eat many vegetables, including zucchini chocolate cake, so I will resist the temptation of further commentary.

Finale

Me and Robert Frost have such love for the English language that we sometimes spontaneously burst into poetry.

Ode to Cattle

A cow gives you milk for your Fruit Loops,
And steaks, liver, tongue, tripe, and brain.
All from a beast that eats grass and poops,
And drools and belches methane.

Discussion Questions

- Why is it that city people do not believe cow-belly magnets are real?
- How do you persuade a cow to swallow a magnet?
- Do cows have wisdom teeth?

---

[1] An ox, by at least one definition, has not had a cruelty-free life.

NOT ALL WE LIKE SHEEP

Occasionally you should invest in a herd of sheep. It is one of those farm projects where you can work really hard and make a few bucks and almost break even. You will also develop a descriptive vocabulary.

Some people like sheep. They think of sheep as peaceful, pastoral creatures walking around in the clover gently baa-ing to one another. These people have the wool pulled over their eyes and have not been subjected to sheep.

What is the truth about sheep? The Bible tells us.

And he said unto them, What man shall there be among you, that shall have one sheep, and if it fall into a pit on the Sabbath day, will he not lay hold on it, and lift it out? Matthew 12:11

. . .And Abel was a keeper of sheep. . . . Genesis 4:2

There we have the truth about sheep, that they do incredibly stupid things, requiring their rescue, usually on Sunday, and sheep were somehow associated with the first murder.

The main problem with sheep is getting them to go where you want them to go. There are different approaches. In the Middle East, the shepherd leads the flock. The sheep actually follow him around. I believe this is one of the miracles left over from Bible days, and I don't pretend to understand it.

In America, farmers herd sheep. It's the law. Can you imagine what American farmers would say if they saw you walking along with a couple of hundred sheep following you?

When I was young, we always had a difficult time herding sheep. I think that the Australians have the best method. They have spotted dogs that instinctively bite sheeps' heels and thus assist humans in the otherwise impossible task of making sheep go in the desired direction. American dogs, at least the dogs I grew up with, had instincts to race into a herd of sheep, barking loudly, until the sheep were widely dispersed. Then off they would go to find dead animal parts to drag home and deposit on the front lawn.

A sheep begins its life as a lamb, a helpless creature that is always born at 2:30 a.m. during a freak snowstorm. Daddy stayed up all night sometimes, acting as midwife. Sheep have evolved to where they need you there to assist in delivery. By sunup, when the sheep decided to stop delivering, we would have, say, twelve happy little lambs, three frozen lambs, and a penko.

A penko is a lamb whose mother doesn't recognize it and kicks it away when it tries to nurse. Ewes sniff at the lambs to find their own, but sheep get sinus infections or something, and occasionally they orphan their young. We brought the penkos into the back porch of the house where we put them in boxes and fed them. We would put some warm milk in a pop bottle, attach a nipple, and force a penko's mouth open to teach it to drink.

After a few days the penkos knew how to drink, and the snow had melted, so we would take them outside with the other lambs. The penkos required milk for several months, and by then they were large and when they saw me coming with milk bottles, they would attack me, rip the nipples off the bottles, and chug the milk. All the lambs loved to play together and practice skills, such as darting and jumping, skills they would occasionally need later in life.

After the surviving lambs had grown a little, my dad would say, "Tomorrow I want you kids to bring the sheep up so we can take care of the lambs." "Take care of" means to cut off their tails and other things. We occasionally had a "hired man" help take care of the lambs and tell us gruesome stories.

<u>Gruesome Stories</u>

The hired man told us that when he was a little boy, he remembered. . .

Editor's note: Please eliminate this section. Although all hired men told essentially the same gruesome stories, they are apocryphal, possibly upsetting to the naive, and need not be included in a tasteful and accurate textbook such as this.

. . .with his teeth.

Meanwhile, back at the farm . . .

The pasture was long and narrow, and the sheep were always at the far corner. They looked at us coming with their feeble-minded, sheepish sort of looks. My two sisters and I would start to herd them toward home, one of us at the rear and one guarding each side. The sheep seemed cooperative. They moved along, baa-ing, toward the open gate near the sheep shed, but when they got about twenty feet from the wide open gate they stopped. “Hey,” they said to one another, “where are we going? I don't understand. I don't know what they want us to do.” Then, a sheep would get a faint idea, “Hey, maybe. . .yes, it has to be. . .they want us to go through that six-inch hole in the fence into the alfalfa field. Yes!” So the one sheep would dart past my diving lunge through the small hole in the fence.

There is a joke about a teacher who asked a boy, “If you had ten sheep, and one of them ran away, how many sheep would you have?” The boy answered, “None,” which was correct.[1] After our one sheep had darted, the rest of the herd simultaneously got the idea, “Hey, we should dart through that large hole in the fence,” and they did.

I have been taught that profanity is the attempt of a feeble mind to express itself forcefully. This is generally true; however, I defy the most able mind to find a nonprofane expression suitable for helplessly watching the launching of a sheep stampede. How about, “Goodness! I am extremely discouraged about this behavioral characteristic of sheep.” No,

---

[1] This is just one example of the scholastic testing bias against farmers.

we have to be more forceful. How about a statement hinting that sheep were invented in the sewers of hell. That is getting close but it isn't brief and powerful enough for a stampede.

Actually, we ought to control our tongues, and, like David, think of the eternal perspective. *"O, God, . . . why doth thine anger smoke against the sheep of thy pasture?" Psalms 74:1*

This stampede procedure would be repeated several times, and finally, a sheep accidentally would decide to bolt through the wide open gate, and all the sheep, with a cloud of dust, would be in the pen.

It wouldn't have been so bad, but we had to gather the sheep a few weeks later for shearing. The lambs were reluctant about entering the pen again.

"NOW what are they going to do?"

"I don't like this."

"I smell sheep dip."

"What are we doing speaking English?"

"Let's make a run for it."

"Quick, into the alfalfa field."

Daddy did the shearing. This was hard work, but Daddy made a contraption with ropes and springs and counterweights to support his back while he sheared all day. We used it to play Peter Pan. He'd grab a sheep leg from the group behind a little canvas curtain, drag the sheep out, sit it on its rump and shear down the belly and then to both sides and around. It was fun to watch. A freshly sheared sheep looks pretty silly, sort of like an old man walking around in his new long johns. After shearing, we would brand the sheep with red paint.

My job was to gather the sheared wool into a bundle, tie it with string, and throw it into the wool bag.[1] This wool bag was a giant gunny sack that we wet in the ditch, tied ears in the

---

[1] Yes sir, yes sir, three bags full.

bottom corners, and suspended in a rack. Our favorite job was to jump down into the bag and tromp on the wool to pack it tightly. It was a challenge to climb out.

When the bag was full, we would sit on a pole lever to elevate the sack while Daddy sewed the top shut and released it. Then we'd suspend another empty bag and play circus on the full ones.

We were glad when it was over. We would head for the house worrying about ticks, with shoes and trousers waxy and smelly from the wool's natural lanolin. A bath was a welcome relief, especially if someone didn't use all the hot water. It was the most impressive bathtub-ring day of the year.

Sometime in the summer, we would rent some bucks and turn them loose among the ewes. Wow! This educational event had to be carefully timed to schedule lambing to coincide with next spring's freak snowstorm.

In the fall, again we rounded up the sheep to send the lambs to market. It was exciting to see the big truck back up to the chute. I got to operate the little door to let the boy lambs go up the chute and the old sheep and girl lambs to the pen. The big truck would finally pull away, taking our lambs to market in Denver where they were sold to packing plants.

People buy lamb because it is very tasty, especially with a little mint sauce and a large piece of blueberry cheesecake for dessert. On the other hand, some people eat mutton, which is meat from an old sheep. Mutton tastes like an old sheep. It is dreadful unless you wrap it in a grape leaf and eat it while watching a belly dancer.

Daddy made a little money on the lambs. The wool he essentially gave away. But he did teach us how to manage animals, how to work hard, and how to use explosive vocabulary words.

Discussion Questions

- Isn't it absurd to ask a black sheep if it has any wool?
- Is sheep dip something you chew or something you serve with potato chips to unwelcome guests? What about dingleberries?
- Why did George Frederick Handel wear a fluffy white wig?
- Why do you receive a sheepskin after graduating from college?
- Which of the following is not a sheep disease: soremouth, overeating disease, stiff lamb disease, bluetongue, chicken pox?

GOAT ON A ROPE

Many people raise goats. Why? I frankly have no idea. Do they catch mice? Do people actually use goat milk for anything other than pranks? Do you know anybody who routinely eats goats and admits it? Depending on how you phrase your comments, you could get thrown in jail for talking about eating a young goat.

In discussing the subject with one of my associates, I discovered that he once had a small farm in Colorado and had a goat. Careful examination of the last sentence will show that the last verb is in past tense. His children tied the goat up to graze on a hill near a cliff. Government studies have shown that grass is always greener at the bottom of a cliff. The goat was intellectually challenged in the subject of geometry, and the rope was not long enough to reach the bottom of the cliff.

He tried to comfort his children by telling them they should have used mouth to mouth resuscitation to revive the goat. It was a very sad event. My theory is that the goat had once been a Judas goat.

Don't raise goats. They smell like goats. They will eat your lingerie off the clothesline, then go hang themselves. Trolls will occasionally wake you up on Sunday mornings asking if you have any goats to eat. Marketing may also be a problem. I am not even sure if Chicago financial markets sell goat-belly futures. You might give them a call.

HAMMING IT UP

Pigs are important farm animals because they convert eggplant, rotten milk, and other garbage into sausage. Pigs spend most of their lives just lounging around grunting at each other, sort of like the guys at the filling station, but they (the pigs) come to life when you bring them a special treat like ground grain and rotten milk.

Pigs even eat coal. We proved this after getting the idea from Daddy, who occasionally commented about our eating cheap Christmas candy: "You sound like pigs eating coal." Being the scientific types, we took some small coal pieces from the coal shed and threw them into the pig trough, and sure enough, the pigs sounded like us eating Christmas candy. Coal is more nutritious and better for your teeth.

If a pig asked you over for dinner, chances are the *pièce de résistance* would be a choice portion of a bovine whose soul hath been ferried over the river Styx. Pigs get to eat the stupid, dead cows that died accidentally, like the ones that bloated on alfalfa or the one that got her head stuck in the hay loader. Daddy was always quite angry with cows that died accidentally. He would pull them with the tractor past the living cows, as an object lesson, to the pig pen where he once asked me to slit open the cow's belly so the pigs could start eating. Kids need to learn the correct way to do these things.

A dead cow was fun for the pigs, but it also attracted magpies from miles around. Daddy paid me five cents per dead magpie because magpies eat pheasant eggs, and their cackling wakes you up in the mornings. They also cruise the highways looking for dead things, putting them in the same category as lawyers. I would sit by the pump house for hours waiting for the cautious birds to approach. Finally one would swoop in, one eye looking at the dead cow, the other eye looking for a ten-year old with a .22 loaded with bird shot. Slowly I would raise the gun, pull back the firing pin, and BANG! Another nest of pheasants saved to grow up into adult birds for me to shoot.

We tried a few times to obtain piglets the natural sow (and boar) way, but when and if piglets did come, the mother usually squished or ate them. There is also the problem of what to do with the runt. Every litter of pigs, just like every high school class, includes a mangy little runt. The other piglets keep locking the runt in his locker, shoving him naked into the awards assembly, and putting milk in his salt shaker. Life is not easy for the runt. The best thing to do with a runt is to give him away to some poor people who will feed him plenty of slop and raise him to become president of a major software company.[1]

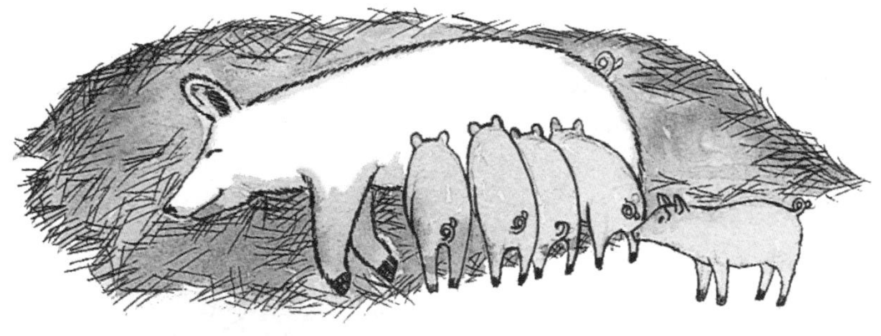

We usually gave up on the sow and went to the auction to get piglets. The auction barn was a fascinating, smoke-filled place with a fenced ring in the center where cattle, sheep, or

---

[1] This is just stereotype satire not meant to make you think of specific people like Ross Perot.

pigs[1] walked around for all to evaluate. With livestock in the ring, the auctioneer, with jowls shaking, would start ranting and raving with occasional inflections, "Heywannawannawanna-FIVEyehwannafiftwannaYEHwannawannaSEVENwannayeye-FOURTHOUSANDwannawannaCOWwassnwagrrlkjoawan-HUNDREDyoyomaYEPwannaklaailoveyouyeahoeeieiOaogive meaHOmeIneedairwa-nnagoatHo." Occasionally he would breathe, and men would then drive in some new livestock. A couple of men in the ring would peer up through the cigarette smoke and occasionally yell, "Yip!" which meant that someone was bidding, but I think they were lying because no one was doing anything, and you couldn't see through the smoke. We got headaches. I think that, besides somehow getting some baby pigs, Daddy wanted to show us the effects of cigarette smoke.

On the way home from the auction, we usually stopped at A&W for a frosty mug of root beer. It became a tradition that lasted until I was a teenager and took some steers to the auction by myself, and I pulled up to A&W, forgetting that the stock racks would rip the awning off the place. I wish I could go back and erase a few things from my life. That would be about number six.

Once the little pigs were in our pen, we began feeding them grain and slop and weeds. After they grew some, we realized that we had better take care of certain details before they grew too big.

Warning! The following paragraph contains graphic descriptions of little piglets squealing so loud you'd think they were being castrated or something.

My job was to hold the squirming rear legs and sit on the piglet's belly while Daddy did his work with a sharp pocket knife. Sitting on a piglet's belly is not the most wonderful place

---

[1] This little piggy went to market.

to sit because that happens to be where wet stuff sprays out, especially when a piggy is experiencing a major surgical event. Still, sitting on the belly seems better than sitting on the head where you might be bitten where you hope you are never bitten. Sitting too near the rear end in also not wise because you do not want to sit too near the semi-controlled surgery for obvious reasons. While all this is going on, the sow[1] is a couple of feet away through the fence, loudly snorting[2] about what she would do to you if she had some Tower of London torture implements. The surgical event's finale was a dash of iodine that sends a piglet into a squirming and squealing frenzy and signals the time to let go.[3] After holding the last piglet, I could let go and waddle in to take a bath.

We were glad that we didn't have to brand pigs, which probably would have set them on fire.

Pigs enjoy playing in the mud, and we often made mud for them by forgetting to turn the water off. At supper Daddy would ask, “Is the pig's water turned off?” and I would have to go out in the dark to the shadowy pump house where the boy-eating-ogre lives at night. I would locate the hazardous knife-switch, which would shock me if I grabbed it wrong, and pull the handle to turn off the water that had now filled the pig pen and was irrigating the entire corral, which is one of the few places on a farm you do not want to irrigate.

The time eventually came to butcher a pig. This event begins with killing the pig, which is not easy if all you have is a .22. I remember watching Daddy shoot the pig between the eyes, and the pig just stood there. The pig finally decided it was dead and fell over, and we commenced to slit its throat and scald

---

[1] Assuming you have a sow.
[2] With an oink-oink here and an oink-oink there.
[3] Oui-oui-oui all the way home.

it in a huge vat filled with hot water. Once scalded, the pig was ready to have its hair scraped off. This process is essential because there is an old farm rule — nothing should be easy or fun. Years later, Daddy decided to just skin pigs, cut up pork chops, and grind everything else into sausage, including the hams. This is because of the smoked-ham-of-doom experience.

Daddy made a smoker from a stove-type contraption with the stovepipe venting into a box where he hung the hams. Smoldering hardwoods give ham the correct, subtle flavoring, so Daddy burned some old apple wood, shovel handles, etc. The ham smoked for several days, and then we hung it up in the cellar. Momma cut some ham off and cooked it, but it had a rather overwhelming taste of apple-tree and shovel handle smoke. She found that by boiling the ham until the smoke flavor was substantially reduced it became edible.

We made the best sausage in the world. The recipe requires a big tub of ground-up pig, salt, sage and a few other things like that. We cut all the fat off the meat before grinding, and it was the leanest sausage I have ever seen. Momma had to grease the pan before frying it.

Momma cooked the fat to make lard for making bread and pie crusts, two things you will eat a lot of on the farm, and soap, which you will only eat after you have been caught using explosive vocabulary words in situations other than herding sheep.

We recycled the innards except the heart, which we boiled and sliced into tasty sandwich meat, good with mustard. We sometimes blew the bladder up using a straw and tied the ends to make a kick-ball that the dog would soon puncture and deposit on the front lawn.[1] See "Farm Decor."

---

[1] We did this because making pig-bladder balls is one of those depression-era stories that we wanted to verify.

With one pig butchered, it was time to take the rest to the auction and buy some new piglets. We wanted to go with Daddy. It was time for some nicotine and a root beer.

Discussion Questions

- Should a pig be allowed to sing the national anthem? What if she is a TV star?
- What are you supposed to do with a pig skin?
- What if the defense is showing blitz?
- Did I tell you the story about Ted and the pig's head?

A farmer of my acquaintance, whom we'll just call Ted, since that is his real name, butchered a large pig. A poor family down the road had requested the head, because many parts of the head are edible, but the family was not ready to take possession of this free tidbit. Ted put a few gunny sacks on top of the frozen food in his freezer and placed the head there, snout up, to await the time for delivery to his poor neighbors. In the cold of the deep-freeze, the whiskers frosted over, and what was once just a bloody pig's head took on the appearance of "the frozen hog's head from hell."

- Do you think, in hindsight, that Ted should have warned his wife?

A HORSE! A HORSE! MY KINGDOM FOR A HORSE[1]

If you own several thousand acres and run hundreds of cows, you must have horses. A good horse helps in "cutting" calves, which, in this case, means separating calves from their mothers (rather than from their potential children). You might also use horses to carry equipment to where you can fish in a clear mountain lake, up where mother nature's defense mechanism makes tourists get altitude sickness. Your horse can help carry elk segments out of the mountains, but we never went elk hunting because we always had sufficient beef in the freezer.

A horse is clearly a useful animal to have around, even on a small ranch; however, there are certain drawbacks to owning a horse. You will find yourself associated with other horse owners, most of whom listen to country western music. Is this the crowd you want to horse around with? I ask you! How many rodeo-bound horse owners listen to classics like Mozart's "Concerto for Flute and Harp" or Elton John's "Funeral for a Friend?" And why don't rodeo announcers demonstrate the same *savoir faire* (appetite for Brussels sprouts) that you expect from horse owners who participate in fox hunting and polo?

Rodeo announcer with *savoir faire:* "For our next equestrian performance Mr. William Robert Weedthorpe will demonstrate his attempt to stay astride a Brahman bull for as many seconds as his estimated IQ. . . . Bravo. . .Bravo. . . . Now while the clowns attempt to recover Mr. Weedthorpe's remains, let's listen to Elton John's 'Funeral for a Friend.'"

---

[1] A famous quote from Shakespeare's *King Richard the Third* signifying excessive hunger.

Pardon me. Let me plummet from my high horse (*haut mulet*) and return to the mane subject, namely the side effects of owning horses.

Horses need constant training. This training consists of two categories: difficult and impossible. For a while we had a pony on our farm, and I would occasionally saddle it and slip the bridle with a split[1] bit onto its head. I wanted to make the pony gallop. This was difficult. I would kick and yell, and the pony would go trot-trot-trot-trot-trot-walk-walk-walk-walk-walk-stop. Then I would yell and kick and repeat the sequence until we were about a half mile from home. Then I would turn the pony around for the next part of the training — making the pony stop galloping.

We also had a horse named Jack, because he looked like a mule. I think he was part mule, although that is genetically rare. Jack was gentle, easy to steer, and a perfect horse for kids. Except for his constant and often successful attempts at biting us. Jack also had a habit of jumping the fence into the neighbor's horse pasture full of quality mares that soon had some not-so-quality offspring resulting in a not-so-happy neighbor resulting in a not-so-fully-equipped Jack.

Discussion Questions

- What does it mean, "horse of a different color"?
- When are the Denver Broncos going to win a Super Bowl?

---

[1] Worthless!

CHICKENS ARE FOUL

Every farm should have a barnyard full of chickens and a rooster to serve as an alarm clock. We always had chickens. In fact, one of my earliest recollections is of being pecked on the eyebrow by a sitting hen. My wound required Merthiolate and a Band-Aid. That was a long time ago, and thinking about it now I just laugh. . .whenever I barbecue.

You may be surprised to learn where chickens come from. Thirty-three percent of high school graduates will tell you that chickens come from eggs. Twenty percent will say, "Like, from the grocery store, you know." Five percent will mention the other side of the road. The rest won't be able to read the question.

The correct answer is Sears. This is a fact. You kids can just call up Sears and charge a box of one hundred baby chickens. (Don't tell your parents. Surprise them on Easter morning.) A cheeping box will arrive in the mail in a couple of days. Once the chickens arrive, you will need a brooder (a cage with a heat lamp in it). Turning these sweet little chicks into chickens is easy. Just add a little water and four thousand pounds of chick feed.

As the chicks begin to grow, they soon develop combs, they start pecking at each other, and scruffy wing feathers replace the cute, soft, yellow fluff. This is known as the teenage stage. Soon they are ready to turn loose in the chicken yard for a raccoon to eat. After you trap and shoot the raccoon, you can wait a few months and begin to harvest the remaining roosters.

Your first challenge will be to catch the chicken. You will need a long rod with a U-shaped hook on one end to grab a chicken's leg as it runs or flies by. An alternate approach, one that I invented as a young boy, is to accidentally leave your fishing pole out in the yard with a worm still attached to the hook. This offers a little more “play” than catching small trout, but it does not offer you the opportunity to select the best size or sex of chicken, unless you are quite skilled at casting.

You may be shocked to learn that before you can eat a chicken, you must personally chop its head off. When I took my Oakland-raised fiancée home to meet the family, she watched from an upstairs window as my mother carried a chicken over to the woodpile and suddenly, “swishchump.” This horrified my fiancée. . .and the chicken. You may choose to wring the chicken's neck as an alternative to chopping; however, this may do psychological harm to other chickens that may be watching. Check local chicken killing regulations.

Scald the headless chicken with boiling water and pluck the feathers. Ah, the aroma of hot, moist chicken with wet feathers stuck to your hands, and hungry cats watching nearby — these are the best of times. Then you must set a paper bag on fire and hold the chicken aloft to singe all the chicken hair off. Yes, friends, chickens have hair. Why else do they need combs?

Editor: “Let's cut down on the sophomoric humor.”

Now you are ready to clean the chicken. You might want to skip this section if you are chicken and have no guts.

Cleaning a Chicken

1) Cut off the feet. A chicken foot is a great toy because you can grab the tendon and pull on it and the claw will open and close. If you like to amuse your dinner guests, you might leave the feet attached sometime.

2) Cut through the skin and tissue around the place where the digestive process finishes, to have access to the guts.

3) Remove what my four-year-old calls “the instructions.”

4) At the beginning of the instructions, you will find a comical purple organ called the gizzard. Cut it open, taking care not to puncture the inner membrane, and peel the gizzard off the inner sack, and save the gizzard.

5) Keep pulling.

6) Remove the craw, a disgusting bag of food and sand that is under the skin at the bottom of what is left of the neck.

7) Reach in and scoop out the liver and heart. Cut off anything disgusting attached to the liver and discard it.

8) Scrape out the lungs and kidneys.

9) Rinse the inside of the chicken several times.

10) Feed the heart, liver, and gizzard to the dog unless you are one of those who actually enjoy eating chicken giblets. (Goes well with lima beans.)

11) Impersonate a chicken clucking and chase your sister around the house with the chicken carcass.

12) Hey! Get that @#%*& chicken out of the living room.

13) Leave the chicken whole to roast or cut it into Kentucky-Fried-Chicken-shaped pieces to fry.

The roosters should all be processed unless you want to keep one to try to get some baby chicks the non-Sears way. I would not recommend this, mainly because of an experience a few years ago when we took our kids to the farm. Our kids like to search the farm and gathered <u>all</u> the eggs for Grandma. A few days after our visit, my sister arrived, and Momma asked her if she wanted a fried egg. What came out was not what it was cracked up to be.

Disease

There are a few minor symptoms to watch for when you raise chickens: incurable disease and cannibalism. Colorado

State University printed an informative pamphlet that begins with the reassuring statement, "Chickens are heir to so many diseases that it's a wonder any of them reach maturity."[1]

The article continues on this positive theme by discussing chicken cannibalism. "In all the years of raising chickens (by the author), the only one real persistent problem has been cannibalism. It usually starts about the time pin feathers begin to appear on the young birds. There can be many causes, but once started it becomes a bad habit[2]. . .Some of the more common causes of cannibalism are crowding, boredom,[3] too much heat, too much light and improper diet.[4]

The whole problem starts when one chicken starts picking at another one, usually in the vent region.[5] She draws blood, and pretty soon all the other chickens are picking at the poor thing. It doesn't take long for the flock to kill her and to keep on picking until all that's left is a rather ghastly mess.[6] They then usually start on another one."

Chickens should not be allowed to eat one other. Otherwise how will they grow up so we can eat them? Happily there is a cure. The chicks can be purchased "debeaked," so they appear unsightly and if a chick glances at another debeaked chick it will turn into stone, or you can put pine tar on the wounded vent region of the target chick. Pine tar tastes terrible and thus discourages cannibalism, but make sure you wash most of it off your hands before playing professional baseball.

---

[1] From "The Homesteader's Handbook to Raising Small Livestock." Reprinted by CSU.

[2] Just in case you thought it might be a good habit.

[3] Chickens should be kept away from daytime television.

[4] Maybe you should add a little chicken meat to their diet.

[5] We appreciate the way the author selects inoffensive nouns.

[6] We pause for a moment of silence.

Foul Behavior

Chickens are prone to hysteria, so never burst through the hen-house door and yell, "I've got you, my pretty, and your little dog too!"[1] no matter how amusing you think it is. Rather, you should "knock several times before opening a door to the poultry house to draw the birds' attention so that they won't be startled when the door opens."[2]

Try to consider how the poor chicken feels. How would you like it if you and your wife are watching *Wheel of Fortune*, and suddenly a seven-hundred pound chicken crashes through your door and yells, "I've got you, my pretty, and your little dog too!" You and your wife might feel the sudden urge to fly to a corner of the room and suffocate.

Eggs

If you have chickens you will have plenty of eggs for you and your skunks to eat. You must gather the eggs each day, clean them, and either eat omelets every meal or find someone who will trade eggs for piano lessons.

I really learned about egg production from visiting Uncle Alfred's chicken farm (not "chicken ranch," which has a disreputable connotation). Uncle Alfred had hundreds of chickens and a neat machine that sorted the eggs (AA, A, D+, Large, Low Fat, etc.).

Uncle Alfred's was always a fun place to visit. Once his son Alvin and I went to the chicken coop and discovered that it was entertaining to throw eggs. They made neat splats on the wall,

---

[1] A line from the classic movie, "*Toto! Toto! Toto!*"
[2] Animal Science Merit Badge book, BSA, p70.

and the chickens flew around like crazy, and soon the coop was a carnival of flying chickens and dust and splatting eggs. I figure that the sound of laughing little boys, cackling, flapping chickens, and splatting eggs was heard as far away as Nebraska. Suddenly the door opened. You could have heard an egg drop.

I will leave it to your imagination as to what happened. This is a technique that brilliant authors sometimes use to end a story. I learned this in second grade when I read a story called "The Lady or the Tiger" where at the end of the story the hero was in a pit, where he had the choice of opening one of two doors. He opened a door and the story ended. What was behind the door? I have pondered this for many years. Was it the beautiful princess with whom he could live happily ever after, or was it Uncle Alfred and Daddy?

Adopt-a-Chicken

I have decided to jump on the nineties bandwagon (as long as they are not playing rap music) and start my own animal protection program as an alternative to the exploitation of chickens.

Meet Henrietta.

Henrietta lives in a cage. She is being fed man-made food pellets so she can be exploited for her eggs. Soon she will be too old to meet her egg quota. Her head will be chopped off and her gizzard pulled out. Henrietta will then be made into delicious chicken enchiladas with blue corn tortillas and green chili sauce. You are invited.

Yes, you are invited to help save Henrietta. If you send me $450 per month, I will save her from this ignominious fate. She will be taken from her cage and be placed in her own six-bedroom house in Carmel, California. Henrietta will be served portions of the best foods known: fresh salad, French bread, 8-oz. prime rib with horseradish sauce, cheesecake, etc. Her eggs will only be used to throw at people coming out of KFC.

Henrietta will be personally flown to Europe and other poultry-intensive continents to visit her distant relatives. She will be one happy chicken. When the day comes that she dies of what appears to be natural causes, she will be flown to Hawaii, cremated in reverent ceremony at the beach, and her ashes will be flung into a planter box at the hotel to bring new life to some of the prettiest flowers in the world. She would want it that way.

We know that you will want to participate in this program so you won't feel guilty for the rest of your life. You will receive a color photograph of Henrietta peacefully roosting in her library at Carmel. We will send you adoption papers so you can claim her as a dependent on your income tax forms.[1] For an extra $34.00 we will send you a fabulous recipe for green-chili chicken enchiladas so you can be reminded of the cruel fate Henrietta is avoiding.

Discussion Questions

- How many baskets should you put your eggs in?
- How does one run around like a chicken with its head cut off? Demonstrate.

---

[1] We are not responsible for accountant and legal fees.

TURKEYS

So, you want to raise turkeys. Well, be advised that turkeys have funny growths on their faces, they peck at you, and in many other respects they are similar to the crowd I was standing in line with while climbing the Statue of Liberty.

You can have Sears deliver white or the traditional charcoal-colored turkeylets. Both are equally obnoxious and hateful.

When you are ready to butcher a turkey, make sure you have several strong people to help hold it while you launch it into eternity, and make sure those several strong people hang around to help pull out the wing feathers. If the turkey's death is stressful (to the turkey), it will tense up, releasing some weird chemical into the blood stream that makes the meat tough. There are various opinions about the proper way to kill a turkey. Perhaps the least gruesome method is to grab the turkey's head, and pour beer down its throat until it is in no condition to drive home. Then chop its head off. I call this the MADD method.

To clean a turkey, just stick your hand into the lower opening and pull out the frozen giblets wrapped in waxed paper.

My friend Terry grew up where they have very large commercial turkey herds to sell during the Thanksgiving and Christmas seasons. So he is still a little rancorous when you mention turkeys. He reminded me of several facts about turkeys that must be included in this book if it is to have any credibility as a world-class farming text.

Terry is a Ph.D. nuclear engineer, so his thoughtful evaluation of turkeys and turkey farming should be carefully pondered. You then, as a beginning farmer will gain much wisdom from his articulate insights contained in the following paragraph.

"Turkeys are stupid."

There is some evidence to substantiate his analysis

- Turkeys are so amazed at experiencing a rainstorm that they gaze upward and drown.
- Turkeys have adapted to deal with cool snaps by suffocating each other.
- Turkeys react en masse to anything you say, sort of like convention delegates.

You: My fellow Americ. . . .
Turkeys: Gobblegobblegobblegobblegobblegobblegobble
You: I am going to vacuum the wallets of the rich. . . .
Turkeys: Gobblegobblegobblegobblegobblegobblegobble
You: . . . which includes anyone who can afford a wallet. . .
Turkeys: Gobblegobblegobblegobblegobblegobblegobble
You: . . . we together will change Washington from. . .
Turkeys: Gobblegobblegobblegobblegobblegobblegobble
You: . . . a place where drug dealers and criminals live. . .
Turkeys: Gobblegobblegobblegobblegobblegobblegobble
You: . . . to a place where I live too.
Turkeys: Gobblegobblegobblegobblegobblegobblegobble
You: . . . so this November. . .
Turkeys: Aaaaaaaaaaaaaaaaaaaaaa . . . (suffocate)

Discussion Questions

- Can you think up a practical joke involving a turkey head?
- What is the difference between a snood and a wattle? Which makes a better sandwich?
- What kind of turkey is your congressman?

MACHINERY

To farm properly you will need tractors, combines, windrowers, and all the associated farm implements. You will need a grain truck and a pickup with a horse trailer for cows. You really also ought to have a backhoe with a front end loader because they are handy for scooping trout out of the irrigation ditch, hauling dead animals to the pigpen, digging enormous holes in the ground to install a septic tank (where your wife planted all her tulip bulbs), and shoveling snow.

Once you have purchased a couple of tractors, you ought to buy all the attachments, such as the manure spreader, cement mixer, fence-post digger, rake, mower, baler, cab, stereo, plow, cultivator, sprayer, howitzer, potato digger, catapult, trailer, hedgehog, scoop, and orange triangle. The orange triangle is an important sign to have displayed on your tractor to make motorists[1] aware that it is a slow moving vehicle.

---

[1] Those with tile grout for brains.

After borrowing up to the gills to buy all the required farm equipment, it is time to buy the family car. This should be a yellow and black Dodge Super Bee with a 383 magnum V8 engine, with hood scoops. This is what you really should buy if you want to help your teenage son feel cool enough to ask girls out; however, in actual practice, you probably will end up buying a Chevrolet van powered by a lawnmower engine.[2] It is cheaper, gets better gas mileage, and it won't have power enough to lay rubber, so tires will last longer.

I was fortunate that, as I approached sixteen, Daddy bought a new family car. It was not the Dodge Super Bee I needed, but it was a Mercedes compared to the van. It was a GMC Suburban, and it had a 327 V8 with enough power that if I really romped on it, I could destroy the motor mounts and disconnect the automatic transmission linkage. It was a fairly nice looking machine until my sister backed it into a tree. We named it "Beast."

We also had an old '53 Chevy named "Sarah Jane" that I could start by pushing it and leaping in to throw it in gear and pop the clutch. My brother still has "Sarah Jane" as a paper weight in his garage.

In spite of not having a Dodge Super Bee, I turned sixteen, which is the legal dating age in certain homes in Colorado, and after rehearsing my lines for several weeks, I dialed a cute girl's phone number. When I was seventeen, I let it ring, and a few months later I spoke to her. Once I introduced myself, it would have haunted me the rest of my life if I had hung up, so I asked her out and she said, in a sweet, sexy voice, "No!"

When this happens you need someone to pour your heart out to, which brings us to the subject of

---

[2] We could have had a V8.

DOGS

If you have a farm,[1] you must have a dog, specifically a dog of only partially known ancestry. All farm dogs are mongrels simply because no farmer is ever going to buy a pedigreed dog just to have it get run over by the mailman or get bred by the neighbor's Doberman-poodle.

Dogs have many farm responsibilities in addition to landscaping, but the most important is scaring away thieves. We had many dogs over the years, and the best two watch dogs were Brownie and Lobo. Brownie was part German shepherd and part hyena. She was a very friendly dog and had a happy smile that, to us, meant, "I love you," but when she wanted to give the same message to strangers, it was interpreted as, "I'm going to tear your ears off and eat them."

Lobo was a good watch dog because he was a part Airedale hound and part timber wolf, and he was about four feet tall and extremely ugly. His most terrifying characteristic was his howl. This was no average howl. It was an eerie, bone-chilling howl like you read about in the classic Sherlock Holmes mystery, "You Ain't Nothin' but a Hound Dog."

Another dog function is to listen to you with fixed attention while you discuss the problems of life. City people go visit the psychiatrist, but when you live on a farm, you have to find a qualified substitute.

Me: "Lobo, what am I going to do? I asked her to go rabbit hunting with me and she said, "No." Why did she turn me down? Huh?"

---

[1] EIEIO

Lobo: "Maybe it's your breath."

Discussion Questions

- What did she mean, "No?"

CATS

"What in hell have I done to deserve all these kittens?"
Don Marquis 1878-1937

Cats are optional farm animals. They are handy to have around to catch mice, which is why God originally made them. In actual practice, however, most cats just loiter around the back door waiting for free food, and they swarm around your feet when you come outside. Cats are fairly useless pets. I could never train cats to do anything except sit around the cow so I could spray milk into their mouths while I milked. Daddy told me to stop that because he would sit down to milk and several hundred cats, some from neighboring states, would show up and make the cow nervous. Nervous cows do nervous things requiring split-second decisions.

It is a basic farm rule that no pets, especially cats, are allowed in the house. The house is where you go to escape from animals. We would have been ridiculed by other farmers if we had ever had a cat named Precious Darling IV that we kept in the house and fed canned cat food containing real meat. Farm cats are named Sawtooth, Medusa, or Pizza, and they are NEVER allowed in the house. They eat leftovers and whatever they can find around the farm plus a little of the dog's food.

As useless as cats are, they are still much better than one of those whiny little Chihuahua[1] animals that some refer to as dogs.

---

[1] Spanish for hors d'oeuvre.

Discussion Questions

- What should you do with stray cats?
- What caliber would you recommend?

FENCES

Before you learn all the specifics of raising things, you must first understand the need for and types of fences. Farmers erect fences for several reasons. A fence marks the boundary between your land and your neighbor's land and keeps your cows separated from your neighbor's cows. A fence, however, does not keep your cows separated from your neighbor's bull, meaning that your fence will not last very long. This brings us to the second reason for having a fence:

Your children need work to do, and repairing fences is an excellent opportunity for them to learn farming skills such as how to avoid high velocity barbed wire. I learned this when Daddy was erecting a new fence, and he told me to go stretch the barbed wire and tie it onto the fence posts. I tied one end of the barbed wire to a distant, well-braced cedar post and the other end to the tractor hitch and pulled the tractor forward to tighten the barbed wire. I thought that the wire would be tight enough when it was perfectly horizontal for the entire two hundred yards. I kept pulling forward. The wire was still on the ground. I pulled forward a little more. The wire seemed awfully tight, but it was not off the ground for very much of the span. I pulled a little more...

SPOING...SPOING...SPOING...SPOING...SPOING! The sound echoed off the distant mountains. When my heart started beating again, I took inventory of my important body parts, and I then realized that tight barbed wire does not mean barbed wire parallel to the ground.

Once you have a good fence around your field, it will prevent a cow that somehow got in the alfalfa from finding a way to get out alive (not that it wants to).

There are several kinds of fences.

Barbed wire - This is wire like they put around prisons, nuclear reactors, and rich people's homes to keep cows out. Barbed wire is made to scratch a cow's nose, dissuading it from walking through the fence. Again, this works only for cows. A bull could easily crash into Fort Knox if it thought it would find a cow in the right phase of the moon inside.

Hog-Wire Fence - This is sort of absurd because it implies that someone makes wire that will confine a hog.

Electric Fence - This is barbed wire that carries a painful electrical charge. The theory is that once a bull gets a good shock on the nose, it will realize that it cannot cross the fence unless there is a particularly attractive cow on the other side. Some things are just worth a good shock on the nose. Warning: During July thunderstorms, all fences are potentially electric.

Chicken Wire - This is used to keep all your chickens in one place so the raccoon will have a better selection.

Reinforced-Concrete Fence - This will sometimes keep pigs contained.

Gates: Once you have a fence, you will need a gate so you can theoretically drive the sheep back out of the grain field. A gate is not expensive to make. Just remember that a good gate should be next to impossible to open and close. This will discourage and sometimes even kill cattle thieves. There are several techniques of gate building that you must understand.

- The hinges should be made of baling wire.
- Wooden gates should weigh at least six thousand pounds.
- Metal gates should be made of various old pipes and machine parts welded together to form a frame to which you attach hog wire.
- A wire gate is a movable section of fence-wire secured on one end to the pivot post. The other end of the movable fence section is attached to a movable post that you secure

to a latch post opposite the pivot post. You should have a wooden lever attached to the latch post to pry around the movable post to help tighten the gate in place. Once you have the gate secured, just release the wooden lever, which will swing around and break your jaw.

How to install a fence post.

If your farm is	this is how you install a fence post	taking	costing
privately owned	dig a hole about three feet deep, bury a 8' cedar post, and tamp the ground with the shovel handle.	20 minutes	$6.25
a corporation	call a meeting for Wednesday afternoon to discuss the critical path plan, to hear a presentation on optimum fence post spacing, and to gaze at boring charts; then assign a plebeian to write a job order for a crew to install the fence post per approved design prints.	4 weeks	$4,800

a government project	issue a contract to a beltway consultant to study the impact of the fence post on nearby wetlands, possible archaeological latrine sites, and endangered subterranean species; then go out for bid with a task to install the fence post by a properly licensed and well-connected contractor in compliance with all federal, state, and local regulations.	9 years	six million dollars
owned by the people (communism)	take your state-of-the-art, envy-of-the-world shovel to the field, then drink vodka and wait for materials to arrive from the ministry of fence posts.	several generations	free, much like universal health care.

Discussion Questions:

- What do little boys dare each other to do to an electric fence?

CROPS

Hay

Daddy was glad to have four boys to help with the hay. Hay requires irrigating, cutting, raking, baling, hauling and feeding to livestock. He did not count on four boys with bad hay fever. We could take antihistamine, and we could be forced to work in the hay field as long as we didn't fall asleep and fall off the tractor and get killed. We helped, but we never did baling, which involves driving along at about 1/8 mile per hour in a giant hay dust cloud so dense it leaves a shadow. If you have hay fever, baling hay makes you feel like you are trapped in an oven in a Shake 'n Bake bag with gnats and ground pepper, with feathers in your nose.

I liked cutting hay because it was not a dusty job and it was an opportunity to now and then chase skunks, rabbits, or snakes with the mower blade.

Once you have baled the hay and it dries you must haul and stack 5,000 bales of hay before it rains that afternoon. Stack the hay while singing ". . .tote that barge, lift that bale. . ." If you can find a banker who won't laugh at you, you can buy an automatic hauler/stacker that will allow you to minimize manual labor so your kids can go fishing while you haul the hay.

We always hauled the hay manually. When I was quite young, I got to drive the tractor very slowly around the field while Daddy and a hired man stacked the bales on the trailer. I did a great job of driving except for not knowing exactly how to avoid driving into fences. In later years my driving skills improved to the degree that I could pull a trailer load of hay across a small ditch with just the right touch on the clutch to cause my brothers to fall to the ground in an avalanche of bales.

Discussion Questions

- What percentage of hay bales contain live rattlesnakes?

Grain

There are several grains that farmers attempt to grow.

Oats are used to make oatmeal, oat bran and straw. Oats are good for cows, other hoofed animals,[1] and irregular people.

Wheat is used to make flour, a key ingredient in Hostess Ding Dongs and other essential foods. Wheat sells for a few dollars a bushel. The exact market price varies, but it is usually less than it costs to produce. The market price is determined by men wearing neckties in Chicago who yell and scream and occasionally hit the bell and yell, "Pit!" Then, wheat is turned into Wheaties that costs several dollars a box. The manufacturer of Wheaties then pays millions of dollars to a major athlete for the box cover. Wheat, therefore, is a very important part of economic growth.

Barley is used for pig food that can also be fermented to make beer.

Corn is the mascot of the University of Nebraska. Its unit is the ear, which includes the husk, silk, cob, kernels, and one of those disgusting worms. Corn is first mentioned in history when the Indians said, "Hey, let's invite the pilgrims over to watch a video[1] and serve them popcorn drenched with coconut oil. Then they will all develop heart disease and die." Unfortunately, the Indians forgot to mention the negative health effects of saturated fats to the Pilgrims, so Americans had to wait until the 1990's to

---

[1] Mares eat oats, and does eat oats, and little lambs eat ivy.

[1] *How the West was Won*

begin dying from theater popcorn. Corn is used today to make automobile fuel and tacos.

Flax is grown for its seeds that yield linseed oil and its fibers that are made into cotton sheets, napkins, and tablecloths.

Beans - This crop is difficult to ruminate tastefully without harking back to those "musical fruit" songs popular among sixth graders. We, however, must try to discuss the subject at a more mature college level. But this makes no sense at all because I remember college students who deliberately ate mass quantities of beans and then engaged in behavior that would make the most obnoxious of sixth graders look like Queen Elizabeth.[1]

Beans are an excellent source of protein and fiber, and I would recommend them to everyone except those who share my tent on camping trips. If you insist on taking beans on camping trips, try this simple recipe/prank that I remember from scout camp. On second thought, I don't want to be held liable.

Bean varieties: Pinto, black-eyed peas, appaloosa, refried, black, green, lima, and chili.

Sunflowers grow wherever you plant other grain to lower the value of your crop. Giant sunflowers grow in your garden and are good for making seeds that you can eat and spit out the shells in school so you can spend time talking to the principal.

To raise grain, you must buy seed grain — grain that has been dipped in pink rat poison.

Before planting the grain you must first fertilize your soil. You can use 1) a manure spreader (machine) that flips clods of dry manure about fifty feet in the air or 2) a manure spreader (cow). The cow does a more concentrated and random job, it is essentially free, and it is the primary source of material for your

---

[1] Not literally, or they would have a very difficult time in junior high school.

manure spreader (machine) anyway. In the fall, just turn your cow herd into the field you want to plow in the spring.

Once, back in the sixties, some hippies announced that they would occupy the park in town to have a love-in. Farmers did not appreciate hippies back in the sixties, to put it mildly, so the day before the love-in, some folks moved in with a convoy of manure spreaders (machines). Then they turned on the sprinklers. Their deposits proved to make the park inadmissible, surprisingly even for hippies. This was a proud day for farming.

A good source of fertilizer is the chicken coop. If you have children, just tell them to go clean out the chicken coop. After whatever it takes to convince them that you are serious, they will go out with shovels and participate in a memorable experience. If I had known as a boy what I know now, I would have refused to clean out the chicken coop. Instead, I would have written a memo to my father.

Dear Daddy,

"Bioaerosols of fecal droppings may cause health-related effects, especially in susceptible individuals. Although rare, a few diseases can be transmitted from bird to man. The infectious elementary bodies are easily aerosolized by infectious birds. The most susceptible population are usually the young and elderly. Here are some Viral, Rickettsial, and Protozoal Infections that have been documented to be transmitted by birds to man:

Viral Infections:

Orthomyuxovirus group (influenza)
Paramyxovirus group (New Castle disease)

Rickettsial Infections:

Chlamydiosis (psittacosis, ornithosis)

Protozoal Infections:

Sarcosporidiosis

Attached for your information are two references which were instrumental in assessing whether this observation should be a health concern."[1]

Love,

Lowell

After fertilizing, you must plow. This is an exciting job but only when compared to watching someone knit a blanket. You must go up and down the field in third gear with the tractor throttle on "very loud." You must constantly adjust the plow depth to turn over the maximum amount of soil without getting stuck and burying the tractor up to the axles.

This balance can change quickly. I occasionally buried a tractor trying to get unstuck. This required another tractor to pull me out and possibly another tractor and a truck or two to help. Daddy was not amused when we buried tractors, so we learned to give up and go get help in the early stages of being stuck.

To avoid boredom I occasionally would set up a fishing pole in the pool below the headgate and periodically drive the tractor over and check to see if I had caught anything. Another time I was plowing near the bee hives, not realizing the honey man had

---

[1] From a memo about CONCERNS WITH LOCATION OF BIRD FEEDERS, written with grim seriousnes, where I work. Careful analysis of this memo reveals that its author is creating the very substance that the memo describes as unhealthy.

just robbed the bees. Freshly robbed bees are not in control of their feelings, and so as I approached the hives, the bees attacked, and one stung me above my eye. This is when I learned that I am allergic to bee stings above my eye. I drove home very fast as my eyes swelled shut, and I burst through the door looking like Rocky in the final round. After I was recognized as a human and then as me, I was rushed to my cousin the doctor who gave me a shot and laughed at me.

Soil is very lumpy and uneven after plowing. Now you must go over the field again with the disc, the harrow, the drag (as in "this is a drag"), the fine-toothed comb, and the ditch-maker, and finally the field is ready to plant. A good farmer's almanac will tell you when to plant, the expected rainfall in your area, and the anticipated wind chill in Buffalo during the playoffs. Planting grain requires the ability to see where you have already planted, and I never could do it. When I planted, it looked as though an Edgar Allan Poe death tractor had drifted aimlessly around the field.[1]

After planting it is time to irrigate. Irrigation water comes from a ditch owned by shareholders who take “turns” using the water. If you forget and accidentally take water when it is not your turn, the “ditch rider” will gently remind you by leaving a horse's head in your bed.[2]

To irrigate you must go out in your field at two o'clock in the morning and direct the water to dry land by making a dam in the field ditch. They call it a dam because that is the word farmers use a lot when they try to make one.

After being irrigated, the grain begins to grow so deer, rodents, sheep, and other animals can eat it. When the grain is nearing maturity it is ready for the hailstorm.

To harvest (assuming there is something to harvest) you must first windrow the grain, cutting it and heaping it into a neat row where it can dry between monsoon rainstorms that you were praying for in the spring. When and if the grain dries, it is scooped up by the combine where, inside, hundreds of little mechanical slaves, singing “Old Man River,” thresh and winnow to separate the grain from the chaff. The grain is augured into a waiting truck that will take the grain to the grain elevator, where you sell it for almost as much as it cost to produce. The chaff

---

[1] Once upon a field dreary, while I planted, weak and weary,
Wondering why I was dubbed to do this tedious chore,
While I nodded, nearly napping, suddenly there came a flapping,
As of some feathered vertebrate, going to gorge some grain galore.
“Tis some worthless magpie” I muttered, “that’s what I brought the gun here for.”
Only this and nothing more.

[2] From “The Godfather”, starring Marlin Brando, Mr. Ed, and Charlie the Tuna; edited for television.

may be baled to make a straw stack as a backstop for archery practice.[1]

On our farm we raised alfalfa and whatever grain would be at rock bottom prices at harvest time. We didn't know how to play the commodity futures market like today's farmers who guarantee before planting that their crop will sell at quite a bit less than the record-breaking prices at harvest time.

Discussion Questions

- What happens when someone yells, “Pit” before they corner the market?
- Should a farmer's résumé contain the phrase “harrowing experience”?
- What is a porkbelly future? Breakfast?
- A kid'll eat ivy too, wouldn't you?

Fruit Trees

You may choose to raise fruit trees on your farm. That way you will be able to make fresh apricot cobbler, fresh apple juice, canned cherries, and other wonderful stuff. The trouble with fruit trees is the time it takes for the tree to reach maturity.

Planting - Dig a huge hole and plant the bare-root or root-ball tree in the hole in such a way that the farm animals can easily chew on it.

Painting - You have to paint the tree trunk white to scare off evil spirits.

---

[1] About 20% of your arrows will hit a gap and disappear.

Pruning - When the tree has branches going every which direction you should get some sharp tool and whack randomly at the branches.

Fertilizing - Every winter you should turn your cows into the orchard.

Harvesting - This seldom happens because it freezes every year just when your tree is in full bloom or, when a tree is finally mature, it will get some kind of fungus blight and die. When you are lucky enough to get a crop of, for example, cherries, you should gorge yourself and really mess up your digestive system. Any remaining fruit should be bottled for the winter.

Seeds

You probably remember from high school biology that each tiny acorn contains all the essential genetic information to make a giant pine tree, but only under just the right conditions. To understand what conditions are ideal, just visit your kid's yearly science fair. There is always an experiment titled something like, "What can you pour on plants to make them grow?" Below the posterboard backdrop there will be seven Styrofoam cups with dead plants in them labeled: 1. Water 2. Milk 3. Vinegar 4. Salt Water 5. Diet Root Beer 6. Drano 7. Nothing. The conclusion will be, "I think water is best unless you forget to do it."

The main parts of a seed:

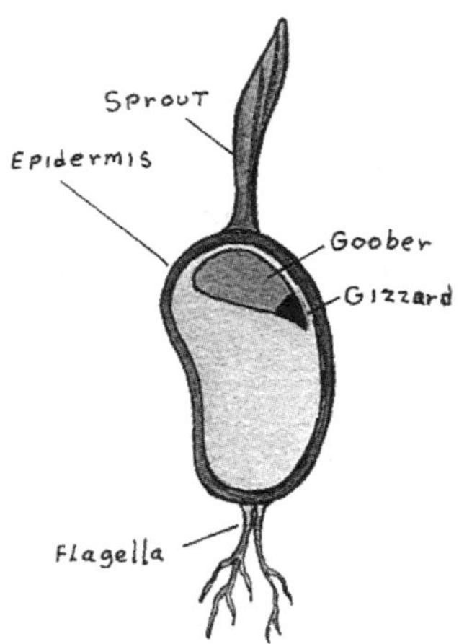

A Child's Garden of Weeds

You must plant a garden to provide fresh peas, green beans, squash, beets, and other nutritious things your children will refuse to eat. Your children can help by weeding the garden. This task makes a wonderful punishment, like in medieval literature, where you weed a row in the garden and turn around to discover that the weeds have all grown back.

You must learn by trial and error what vegetables grow well in your area. Zucchini grows everywhere, and when you forget to pick one it grows large enough to carve into a canoe.

In Colorado, certain plants such as corn do well in spite of weeds, until the ears are eaten by raccoons. Cauliflower and cabbage do well if you dust them regularly with toxic chemicals. Green beans do well, but who gives a hoot? Squash is a fun plant because you can cut off a leaf stalk and slit the end just right to make an obnoxious honking horn by blowing on it. Fresh turnips are tasty, but the last time I ate several turnips I could relate to how cows feel after eating tons of green alfalfa.

Of course, the most important reason for a garden is as a source of earthworms for fishing.

In spite of the weeds, hail, rabbits, bugs, and high-jumping cows, we usually got quite a bit of food out of our garden. Momma would can or freeze much of the produce so we would have plenty of nutritious food to refuse to eat during the winter.

You should learn how to can vegetables, but this involves learning how to operate a pressure canner. This is basically a huge container that could blow up and destroy your kitchen unless you watch it carefully (meaning never put your children or husband in charge of watching it, especially during the playoffs). Rule of thumb: People who routinely use pressure cookers are people with lima bean stains on the ceiling.

Kitchens are dangerous places. Once my college roommate was out fixing his car and asked my other roommate to check on the eggs that were boiling on the stove. My other roommate promptly forgot and went to study in the library for several hours. Never boil eggs for several hours, especially without water.

Discussion Questions

- What could you do with an eggplant and an M-80?

Gardening Techniques

There are three popular types of gardening: high tech, organic, and "to heck with this."

High Tech

High-tech gardening makes use of modern science which has blessed us with toxic bug killers, genetically engineered tomatoes, tomato seeds in orbit, Agent Orange, Miracle Gro, and other gardening miracles.

Toxic Bug Killers

Toxic chemicals aren't what they used to be. In the old days you could go down to the mercantile and buy chemicals and just loosen the bottle cap to kill all forms of life within thirty yards. It was insect against Rambo. Now chemicals have to be tested to make sure they are environmentally friendly. This is another way of saying that they don't work very well. Now it is insect against Richard Simmons.

To select the best toxic chemical, go to the garden center and find the isle where you have difficulty breathing. Choose the bottle with a label featuring the grossest looking bugs. Carefully read the instructions.

Warning: Do not use on pets, humans, bees, velociraptors, evergreens, mammals, and food.
Active Ingredient: Dimethyl-triethyl-1,2cisboombah-trichloro-polycyclops-transalkyl-mercaptan-mercaptan.
Inert ingredients: Crystal clear Rocky Mountain spring water.
Trade name: Bug-Be-Bombed.
Storage: Store away from all living things.
Directions for use: Put one tablespoon in one gallon water. Spray on plants when you first see or hear insects. Do not breathe while spray is present. Avoid touching plants for several months.
Cleanup: Rinse sprayer, exposed body parts, and pets with tomato juice and baking soda. Burn clothing exposed to spray.
Special precautions: Wear a yellow rubber suit with a supplied breathing air respirator.
Note: Not responsible for mutations.

A better route is to use natural insecticides. These are not the synthetic, highly toxic, complex, organic chemicals made by Ortho. These are the natural, highly toxic, complex, organic chemicals that the Romans served their associates on pizza. "I want a large, pan pizza with pepperoni au botulism endotoxin or olives, poisonous mushrooms, hemlock, and (the coup de grâce) processed cheese. To go."

Tomato Science

Much of the high-tech gardening research deals with the tomato. Home grown tomatoes are juicy, tasty, and nutritious, but those in the stores are 95% plastic. For this reason much research has gone into making a good store-bought tomato, so far without success.

Several years ago even NASA was curious about tomatoes. They wanted to understand the effect of space radiation on tomato seeds. This is an important issue because in Houston it's too hot and humid to go outside and do real work.

Realizing that taxpayers would be equally curious about what happens when tomato seeds are exposed to radiation, NASA sent into orbit a school-bus-sized satellite plastered with tomato seeds. Years later the seeds were retrieved and sent to schools around the country. The schools were instructed to have children plant the seeds to see if any teenage mutant tomatoes would develop. Most kids were thrilled to have anything to do involving the word mutant, but parents were a little skeptical. "What if the seeds are radioactive?" the parents, demonstrating the scientific aptitude of sardines, would ask.

Let me take a moment to explain the difference between irradiated and radioactive. I call this the Little Bighorn example. The Indians were radioactive. Custer was irradiated. So, you can see that tomato seeds that have been irradiated are basically full of holes and harmless unless you eat one and get some of the little arrows stuck in your teeth.

You also ought to know that the radiation in space is exactly the same kind of radiation you deliberately get zapped with at the beach, but at the beach you get less of a dose because you are protected by a lifesaving layer of smog.

The thing that worried people was the possibility that all that irradiation scrambled the genetic information in the tomato seeds so that instead of growing tomatoes, the seeds might produce something mutant and disgusting like eggplant.

The results of NASA's project are fascinating. My dedicated research team[1] discovered that most of the seeds were eaten by gerbils and cockroaches or destroyed by vandals. Others were killed because the teacher (and I want this teacher for MY kids) "didn't realize he had to water them."

Probably the most terrifying results came from a teacher who said cockroaches BROKE INTO HER GREENHOUSE and ate her Earth-based plants, but not her space-based plants. This calls for more NASA questions: Don't you hate it when you hear one of them giant roaches trying to get out of your toaster? Have you ever tasted a tomato plant? Hey! What would happen if ROACHES were sent into space? Taxpayers need to know.

Jurassic Tomatoes

There has been much debate about genetically engineered tomatoes. Scientists have altered the genetic code of tomatoes so they will stay fresh longer and taste better and possibly attack people in their Jeeps and eat them.

---

[1] Sisto Garcia, electrician, reading the *Albuquerque Journal* during his morning break.

Organic Gardening

Organic gardening relies on non-toxic, environmentally kind, and usually worthless bug control techniques.

Soapy water.

If you spray soapy water all over your bug infested garden, some of the young bugs will start screaming, "Mommy, I have soap in my eyes, Aaaaaahhhhhhh! Aaaaahhhhhh! Aaaaaaaaahhh!" and they will make such a scene that the parent bugs will take them into your neighbor's yard and scold them. The idea is that your neighbor will spray them with toxic chemicals, and they won't return to your yard.

Plant marigolds around your garden.

This technique makes the bugs think, "Hey, this is just a patch of marigolds, so let's go next door to the neighbor's vegetables where we will be sprayed with toxic chemicals and die." This method is usually ineffective because insects do not think in compound sentences.[1]

Pour boiling water all over the bugs.

This will kill any bug that you hit, and it will blanch the vegetable for freezing.

Plant extra.

This technique requires you to plant about six acres of cabbage so there will be enough for the bugs and for yourself.

---

[1]Madonna is a possible exception.

To Heck With This

Go into your garden with a machete whacking at every insect you see while screaming, “I can't stand this any longer. I hate you! I hate you! I hate you!” This will attract the attention of your neighbors who will probably call the police.

Composting

Composting is an important part of organic gardening because instead of using synthetic fertilizers you use decomposed garbage that is rich in nitrogen, rodents, and large bugs.

First, build a couple of bins out of boards and chicken wire. Throw all lawn clippings, uneaten vegetables, squash and cantaloupe seeds, moldy jicama, tree leaves, and wormy tomatoes into the bin and mix in a little dirt to stimulate aerobic decomposition. If you put a bunch of lawn clippings in without dirt there will be anaerobic decomposition, and your neighborhood may have to be evacuated due to the odor. This may upset your neighbors, and you want to keep on good terms with them so they will answer the door when they see you coming with excess zucchini.

Not all organic matter is meant for composting. Avoid throwing in things such as railroad ties, silk flowers, Jimmy Hoffa, hemlock, etc.

Every spring take the composted material and roto-till it into your garden. This will assure you of having a garden covered with cross-bred, mutant squash plants.

Helpful Gardening Hints - From my County Agent

Hair Balls

You can keep deer out of your garden by hanging up "small net bags filled with human hair. They seem to be effective when deer pressure is low."[1] In other words, if there aren't very many deer around, hair balls have a good chance of keeping them out of your garden. Hair balls should also keep giant tree sloths away from the Mojave Desert.

Moby Soap

For those of you who want to be politically correct and friendly to the planet but still kill certain insects, one product that has been proven effective is "whale oil soap."[2]

Natural Enemies

If you want to get rid of caterpillars, just fill your back yard with "wasps" and "spiders."[3] After the caterpillars are gone you can always kill the wasps and spiders with toxic chemicals.

---

[1]*Coping with Deer in Suburban Gardens,* New Mexico State Cooperative Extension Service.

[2] *Natural Insecticides for Organic Gardeners,* Ibid.

[3] *Beneficial insects and other arthropods in the yard and garden,* Colorado State University Cooperative Extension.

Discussion Questions

- What was the theater crowd reaction during *Jurassic Park* when Tyrannosaurus Rex ate the lawyer? Explain.

MAKING MONEY

One of the first things you will discover as you begin to farm is that you have no money. Don't be alarmed. This is normal. You must borrow some money from a bank, the FmHA or someone named Vito. Vito will be friendlier, at least at first.

Let me describe banks so you will feel at ease about going in and begging for money. A bank is a building with an enormous lobby with a few people sitting around at empty desks. The people sitting at the desks will ignore you. You must first stand in line to see the young teenage girl behind the counter. She will tell you to go see someone sitting at a desk. After you wait for a person at the desk to finish playing solitaire on her computer, she will instruct you to go sit outside the office of a vice-president. Vice-president is a title given to anyone wearing a suit. The vice-president, if he is in the office, will eventually let you come in and sit across the desk from him. He will talk to you in a condescending manner.

He will have you fill out some inane forms and then have you return several weeks later. Then he will lend you some money if you have enough land and equipment that he can seize if you don't pay up.

If you have no collateral, he will call in all the other vice-presidents, and they will all laugh together for a long time and then tell you to go away.

I once went to a bank when I was a senior in college and asked for a small loan to buy a few luxury items such as oatmeal. The vice-president told me I couldn't have a loan because I didn't have a full-time job. I pointed out to him that if I had a full-time job, I wouldn't need a loan. I wanted to pelt his three-piece suit with eggs, but Uncle Alfred and Daddy might have burst through the door.

Because farmers have historically thought of bankers in the same high regard as horse thieves, farmers have needed another source of money. The Federal Government has lots of money, or at least it is allowed to pretend it does, and a federal agency was created to lend money to farmers. The FmHA built fancy offices throughout the land where farmers can go, fill out some forms, talk to a condescending loan officer, and get money if they have enough land and equipment that can be seized if they don't pay up. The distinguishing feature of FmHA loans is that they require filling out mounds of incomprehensible government forms.

The FmHA forms can be separated into two categories:

- Forms that prove you are a total goober, thus explaining why you desperately need money after years of farming, and
- Forms that prove you are the exact opposite of a total goober,[1] thus explaining how you are capable of paying all the money back.

Once you have the forms complete, you should go to the FmHA to get some money.

The Wrong Approach

You: Howdy. I think I have these here forms filled out, but I didn't understand some of the questions.

Mr. Marley: Come back after lunch when I'm not here.

[1] An incomplete goober.

The Correct Approach:

You: Howdy! I think I have these here forms filled out, but I didn't understand some of the questions.

Mr. Marley: Don't you worry about a thing. Your loan is already approved. By the way, we sure like that new house you gave us next door to the county commissioner.

Once you have money you can purchase equipment, seed, and livestock to help you produce almost enough money to pay the interest on the loan. You have, by now, probably asked yourself, "But how can I make enough money to pay off interest on my loans and still have enough money to replace the pair of shoes that my kid put in the oven?" Take a minute to decide the best answer:

A. Become a doctor and use the farm as a tax write-off.
B. Join a pyramid sales company and fill your garage with soap.
C. Don't plant anything.
D. Stop buying luxuries, such as shoes.

If you answered "C," you are obviously familiar with a popular government program designed to help farmers make a profit. The government will pay you money not to plant anything. If this sounds stupid, then that proves that it is a well-established government program.

Governmental Regulations

In addition to wasting money, the U. S. government has the important job of regulating all aspects of life.[1]

Farming is now included in the government's list of everything to regulate, so you, as a farmer, should keep up on all the new farm programs and regulations just to reassure yourself that your tax dollars are well spent on such things as federally mandated potato-size requirements. You can read about these and other fascinating regulations in a document called the *Federal Register*, a publication that documents the daily regulatory bodewash coming out of Washington, DC.

I will give you a brief look at just one regulation, 7 CFR Part 948 FV-89-012, to argue that Federal regulations have purpose and value. 7 CFR Part 948 FV-89-012 has to do with the Minimum Size Requirement for Certain Long Potato Varieties grown in the San Luis Valley in Southern Colorado. But you might ask, "Why is the Federal Government using my

[1] Including death.

tax dollars to dictate Southern Colorado Potato Sizes?" This is answered in the 7 CFR Part 948 FV-89-012 Summary:

"This interim final rule reduces the minimum size requirement for certain long potato varieties from 2 inches to 1 7/8 inches in diameter. This action is expected to foster increased consumption[2] and have a positive impact on the industry."

Discussion Questions

- What the heck does "interim final" mean?
- Who gets to measure the potatoes? Do you see a possible career path?
- Why don't we pay the British to set Washington, DC, on fire again?
- And how is this regulation going to affect spud consumption?

A Scientific Poll

After reading this regulation, I was a little skeptical about the effect it would have on potato consumption, so the next day I took a poll of the two secretaries downstairs.

Me: May I ask you a question about your potato consumption?

Betty: WHAT?

---

[2] Tuberculosis?

I read them the summary of potato-size regulations. Then I asked, "How will this important regulation affect your potato consumption?"

Janice: I only buy little potatoes.
Betty: I like those new potatoes. . .with parsley and butter.
Janice: And onions. . .with a cream sauce. . . served with some iced tea with lemon.
Betty: And something off the grill.
Janice: And some fresh rolls.
Betty: And a mixed berry pie. . .boysenberries and blueberries.
Janice: With ice cream. . .Haagen-Dazs.

Conclusions:

- Janice and Betty were hungry.

Discussion Questions

- What do French people mean by "*Haut potato?*"
- Why doesn't Betty bring in some mixed berry pie tomorrow?

A Taxing Experience

Once each year, you must take the bull by the tail and do your taxes. Many farmers are intimidated by this process which involves trying to comprehend Schedule F, Profit or Loss from Farming, and Form 4797 for involuntary conversions (which probably has something to do with your son joining the Moonies).

I have studied the tax code for several minutes, and, based on my research, I believe that you should calm down and not worry about taxes, for a couple of reasons:

- You probably have a taxable income about $20,000 below the poverty level.
- I can't think of another reason.

If you do not have time or patience to do your taxes, or if you are dead,[1] you should pay large sums of money to a tax expert, like me, to do them for you. Really though, I would suggest that you do your own taxes, especially after I share this information with you, free, with the purchase of this book.

Answers to the Most Common Farm Tax Questions:

Q. If I am audited, what records will the auditor need to look at?
A. Everything you have written on your barn wall.

Q. I am an asparagus farmer, and I wonder if I should deduct or capitalize the preproductive plant period expenses.
A. Asparagus is a weed.

Q. I bought some calves last spring, but my wife cleaned out the pickup and threw away the receipt. How do I know what number to report as the purchase price?
A. Do you remember learning about imaginary numbers in high school?

---

[1] Refer to IRS tax guides for how to pay taxes if you are dead.

Q. What does the form mean by “Other Expenses”?
A. This is for expenses associated with your dog biting the law student, who swerved to avoid your cow and smashed his Mercedes into your mailbox-on-a-plow that was too close to the road.

Q. Can I deduct the gas and electricity used by my hot tub as business utilities?
A. Yes, if you allow your cows to drink out of it.

Q. What do they mean by “bad debts”?
A Yours.

Q. I sold my entire herd of chickens at midnight on December 31. Do I report the income from the sale on last year's or this year's tax forms?
A. Herd of chickens?

Q. Sure, I've heard of chickens.
A. No, no, no! A chicken herd.

Q. What do I care what a chicken heard? I've got no secrets from an eavesdropping chicken.
A. I think farmers should worry more about eavesdropping pigeons.

Money for the Kids

Since you, as a farmer, will barely scrape by, you should encourage your children to make money on their own to buy things they need, like glass eyes for taxidermy, fish hooks, Cracker Jacks, .410 shotgun shells, and an occasional pizza. When I was a kid, I tried several money-making projects. I made money picking up freshly-dug potatoes, but I quickly figured out that people who do that usually progress on to more prestigious jobs, such as ringing the bells at Notre Dame cathedral.

I tried selling earthworms to fishermen, but I did some rough calculations indicating that is probably not how the Rockefellers made it big. I needed a new source of income.

I ran into the house one day and told Daddy that there was a huge beaver in the barn. He ran out to the barn with me and shot the beaver, which turned out to be a small muskrat. I had never seen a muskrat. This led to my short venture into the fur business. I set traps in the ponds for muskrats. I trapped a weasel, and sometimes I would trap *animal du jour* at the hole in the haystack. I sold furs to a local trapper for a few bucks each.

Discussion Question

- Does the name Quasimodo ring a bell?
- What should you do when you pull the trap out of the haystack with an unhappy skunk attached?
- Then why the heck didn't you do it?

HUNTING

When you become a farmer, you must know how to use a gun so you can kill things, like wolves and pterodactyls, that threaten your livestock. You can also hunt animals for sport, meaning "to put a morsel of food on the table," which is how thousands of non-natives justify their annual trips to Colorado in their motor homes towing Jeeps to hunt Colorado (real) deer and elk.[1]

I grew up during the great jackrabbit boom caused by the shortage of wolves and pterodactyls. The population of jackrabbits was so high there were traffic accidents from drivers trying to avoid hitting them on the highways. So someone offered twenty-five cents per rabbit for mink farm food, and people began to have traffic accidents trying to hit jackrabbits. For a young farm boy, running down jackrabbits was a great way to earn money. I also hunted for them, sometimes during the day and sometimes spotlighting at night. The trick was to kill the rabbit using just one shotgun shell. Two shells was just breaking even, and three meant I needed glasses (which helped).

My favorite hunting was during pheasant season, which, on our farm, meant whenever I decided to hunt pheasants. Pheasant hunting involved stalking through the oat field, eyes alert, trigger finger ready, gun poised while my trusty hunting dog with generations of natural instincts was thrashing through the field about a quarter of a mile away flushing all kinds of pheasants. After about half an hour, I would be walking along muttering about the dog, daydreaming about picking up my date in my new Dodge Super Bee with a 383 magnum V8 with hood scoops, when, from directly between my shoes, a cock pheasant would burst into the air with the sound of Uncle Alfred's chicken

---

[1] Often confused with donkeys and cows.

coop under hyena attack. By the time I raised the gun to shoot, I realized that I had been legally dead for several minutes. I never killed very many pheasants.

I occasionally hunted for ducks, but ducks taste like mud unless you prepare them with complex French recipes that require several days just to decipher the directions. See the appendix.

Discussion Questions

- Do you think the Dodge Super Bee with a 440 engine would be more impressive?
- Don't you think it's overkill to go dove hunting with a 12-gauge?

A FISH IN HAND IS WORTH TWO IN THE BUSH

Farmers need to unwind, and as Shakespeare said, "Forsooth, I think I'll go fishing this afternoon.[1]"

A farm boy must learn to fish at an early age, so when he is older he will take off into the high mountains to fish for several weeks during hay-hauling time.

When I was little, Daddy made a fishing pole - a willow branch with nylon sewing thread attached. He threaded a worm onto the hook and told me just where to plop the bait. I sat and waited while he went back into the house. Suddenly I felt a yank, and I saw a fish dangling from the end of the string. Daddy didn't tell me how to land a fish, so I just sat there with the fish dangling a few inches above the water until Daddy happened to drive by on his way to irrigate. We hauled the monster eight-inch fish in, and a new hobby was born.

I loved fishing. I was very patient and would sit for hours waiting for just the right bait to attract just the right fish. In the fall the water in the irrigation ditches diminished and became shallow and clear, so we could see the fish. My brothers and I would try to put a worm directly in front of a fish's mouth, but it would not bite. Eventually my neighbor taught us that you can just maneuver a treble hook under the trout's mouth and snag him, a process known as "slightly illegal." We later learned to catch trout with our hands, and that was a blast. We would locate trout hiding in the rocks or headgate boards and skillfully grab them and throw them out onto land. Daddy caught fish with pitchforks or the backhoe.

---

[1]From "Shakespeare, the Unauthorized Autobiography, pp.126-128"

Big Bird

One day at school in band class, just before the bell, a fully uniformed game warden strode into the room and asked for Lowell Christensen. All my friends and several cute girls were watching. They believed that the game warden had arrested me, and would send me to a deep dungeon somewhere for all my illegal hunting and fishing activities. This was major negative publicity, an important factor in building high self-esteem among teenagers. I knew immediately why the game warden took me out of school and marched me to his car and drove away with me. It had to do with something the Fish and Game Department takes very seriously. He had come for the eagle.

We had found a dead bald eagle out in our plowed field. It was a huge bird with a wing span of over six feet. We brought it home and showed it to everyone who came to visit. I stored it in the meat cooler in the barn, and I asked the Fish and Game Department if I could keep it and mount it. I was, after all, a graduate of the Northwestern School of Taxidermy, meaning I had read the books they had sent in the mail, but Momma had discovered some of my hideous, sort-of-stuffed birds that, upon completion, resembled pterodactyls, and she at once recommended that I call the Fish and Game Department about the eagle.

The game warden informed me that it was illegal for me to keep the eagle. It would be given to Indians who use the feathers for making nifty ceremonial headdresses. I didn't mind. One of my best friends at school was an Indian.[1]

The game warden brought me back to school where I informed my friends that he had confiscated an illegal bird from where I had hidden it, and as punishment he had brought me back to school in time for P.E.

---

[1] I believe he still is one.

We had a P.E. teacher named "Spanky" Valdez who made us do sit-ups out in the alfalfa stubble, and he kept telling us to keep our butts down during push-ups because the taxpayers driving by were watching. Sometimes he made us have blindfolded boxing matches. Sometimes we would try to fake death to get out of P.E.

Discussion Questions

- Do you think the Northwestern School of Taxidermy is a stuffy school?

RURAL DRIVING

You must familiarize yourself with the subtleties of rural driving. For example, let's say you are driving about seventy miles an hour down a rural lane and you see two headlights ahead in the distance. WATCH OUT! Those are actually the reflections off the eyeballs of a black Angus bull standing in the road about fifty feet in front of you. See, you must learn to drive differently in the country. The biggest challenge is trying to figure out a farmer's driving maneuvers.

The Farmer Left Turn

Farmers have a great fear of being smashed while turning left, probably because they sometimes get smashed while turning left. To protect himself from the other guy, a farmer will suddenly swerve into the far left emergency lane or roadside about a quarter mile from the left turn, travel up to the intersection on the far left and turn left. Another left turn technique is to swerve into the extreme right lane or roadside just before turning and wait for all cars to clear the intersection before making a long left turn.

This is in contrast to driving in Boston where drivers making left turns always have the right-of-way.

The Farmer Right Turn While Thinking About Barley Prices

This turn was invented by my uncle who 1) was driving down the road, 2) waved to the engineer of the train, and 3) immediately turned right, 4) heard a loud noise, and 5) found himself being pushed along the railroad tracks sideways in a smashed truck. Luckily, he survived both times he did this.

The Farmer Concentrating on the Road

When you drive with a farmer you may get a little nervous, thinking that he is not watching the road. Well, relax. You can always tell the farmer is concentrating on the road by the comments he is making. "It looks like Henry's cow had twins. Hmmm. I wonder if he knows they're in his oats. Or are they on the other side of the fence? Them oats look a little dry. Course maybe that's him over there irrigating."

Signals

You need to understand farmer driving signals.

- Left turn signal is on - This indicates that the farmer's left turn signal is still on.
- Hand is held out the window at 90 degrees - Farmer is waving to someone, maybe even you.
- Hand is pointing straight out the window - Farmer is pointing at a coyote.

- Gun is pointing out the window - Farmer is shooting a coyote from the comfort of his pickup cab. Do not pass.

Livestock

You must also learn how to pass a herd of livestock on a rural road. Let's say you are driving your shiny new convertible sports car north and Farmer Jones is driving his herd of sheep south. This is easy. Just park and let the sheep walk around, over, and through your car until the herd is past.

If you and the sheep herd are moving in the same direction you will end up driving in an odoriferous dust cloud about one quarter mile per hour for several days trying to get through. This is a common cause of insanity in rural America.[1]

Cows tend to get out of the way a little better than sheep, but cows are curious animals and as you make your way through a herd of cows on the road, you will get lots of cow drool and other odious substances on your car.

---

[1] In humans. Sheep are already insane.

FARMING IN THE FUTURE

At Epcot Center in Florida there is a ride from the Futureport through a building called "Horizons" where I learned that, in the future, farmers will be made out of plastic. In the meantime, farmers must pay attention to leading agricultural experts such as me, or they will be left in the dust. I have spent several minutes thinking up the following Farming Megatrends, which, if you read them repeatedly, will help you retire early. (Probably before the 10 o'clock news.)

Trend #1.

As you know, consumers are becoming concerned about where their food comes from, which makes you wonder why they eat eggs. Farmers should capitalize on this consumer awareness and, when selling produce, use advertising labels such as "Organically Grown." For example, Organically Grown Mushrooms.

Trend #2.

Consumers, especially health-food enthusiasts, are becoming concerned about what food does not contain. Farmers should market their produce with this in mind.

"Our farm-fresh carrots have not been sprayed with phosgene."

"At last! Fat-free lettuce."

Trend #3.

Farmers will continue not to purchase GQ magazine. This trend will obviously change when farmers are made out of plastic.

Trend #4.

The Baby Boom generation is aging. Just look in the mirror. Depressing isn't it? Farmers who are on top of things will adjust their crops to coincide with the appetites of the Boomers. If I were, for example, raising artichokes, I would rip them up right now and plant prune trees.

Trend #5.

Consumers will continue to be confused about how to eat kumquats.

Trend #6

Computer science will soon make it possible to converse with our domestic animals.[1] I know this because I read a newspaper article, "Researchers Eavesdrop on Pigs." The article quotes Jim DeShazer, an agricultural engineering professor at the University of Nebraska-Lincoln.[2] He has established that "hogs make different sounds identifiable with greeting humans, romancing mating partners, hunger, stress, and other conditions." He determined there is "a single peak to a sound wave emitted by a sow during nursing and a double peak to the sound while giving birth." He concludes by saying, "Microphones and sound-measuring devices could summon a farmer to help when a sow gives birth. . ."

It will not be too long, and you could be in a box seat at the ballet. Suddenly the manager interrupts you and hands you a portable phone. "It's your pig."

"Beatrice, Is that you?"

"Oui."

---

[1] Pending governmental approval.

[2] You wouldn't expect this type of research at Harvard.

"Are you in labor?"

"Oui! Oui! Oui!"

You whisper to your associate, "My sow is in labor. I have to go."

"I understand. I'm expecting a call from my Holstein cow any minute."

Discussion Questions

- Why don't ballerinos[1] wear basketball shorts or something?

---

[1] A male ballerina.

SUMMARY

Having read this definitive work on farming, you must ask yourself these questions to see if you have the right stuff to be a successful farmer.

1. Do you understand that to make money, you must ask the government to give it to you for not planting corn?
2. Do you have skills that will enable you to get part-time employment to supplement your farm income? (Are you a brain surgeon?)
3. Do you find it absurd that some people recommend counting sheep jumping over a fence to cure insomnia?
4. Do you like to eat steak? Almost every day?
5. Fill in the blank. The only good coyote is a _ _ _ _ coyote.
6. Can you catch fish with a pitchfork?
7. Can you drive your combine down the road in such a way that it is impossible for anyone to pass you?
8. Can you throw a hay bale eight feet in the air?
9. Can you think of five hundred uses for baling wire?
10. If your truck bumper rusts off, can you install a new one? (Hint: See question #9.)

Farming is a wonderful profession, and if you answered "yes" to these questions, it is obvious to me that you really blew question # 5. It also tells me that you have what it takes to enjoy. . .

A DAY ON THE FARM

Schedule:
Get up.
Build a fire in the kitchen stove.
Get dressed.
Tell the kids to get up.
Milk the cows.
Feed the calf
Separate the milk.
Feed the pigs.
Chop the ice out of the stock tanks.
Take hay out to the beef cows.
Feed the horse.
Chop wood.
Fill the woodbox.
Tell the kids to get up.
Wash the milk buckets and cream separator.
Eat breakfast:

- Bacon
- Eggs
- Oatmeal
- Canned peaches
- Toast and peach jam
- Milk
- Orange juice

Tell the kids to get up.
Take apart the tractor engine.
Drive to town to get a timing chain.
Drive to another town to get a timing chain.
Stop and talk with neighbor fixing his fence.
Help him drive your bull and his cows out of his wheat field.
Eat dinner:

Roast beef
Mashed potatoes
Gravy
Canned green beans
Homemade bread
Corn on the cob
Stewed apples
Jell-O with sliced bananas and whipped cream
Cheese
Mincemeat pie

Tell the kids to feed the chickens.
Put the tractor back together.
Fix the hole in the chicken fence.
Set traps.
Grind some grain.
Remind the kids to feed remaining chickens.
Try to find hack saw.
Ask kids where hacksaw is.
Borrow hacksaw from neighbor.
Try to remember why you needed a hacksaw.
Eat supper:

Biscuits and honey
Canned peaches
Milk
Carrot sticks

Milk the cows.
Feed the calf
Separate the milk.
Feed the pigs.
Feed the horse.
Wash the milk buckets and cream separator.
Tell kids to go to bed.
Watch the 10:00 news.

Mutter uncomplimentary remarks about Congress.
Go to bed.
Go almost to sleep.
Tell the kids to go to sleep.
Go to bed.
Ask the kids if they fed the chickens.
Get dressed.
Feed the chickens.
Go to bed.
Realize that the chickens are asleep and you didn't really have to feed them.
Go to sleep.
Get the 12 gauge and shoot at the raccoon in the trash barrel.
Go to bed.
Go to sleep.

APPENDIX

I have included a few recipes to teach you what to do with farm products you normally throw away, like dead ducks, cow accessories, and zucchini.

Roast Duck Flambé a la Hastings de Kumquat et Mud Gout

According to my library research, this is the meal that inspired William "Bill" the Conqueror to leave France.

Ingredients:
1 dead duck
1 teaspoon salt
1 teaspoon pepper
1 cup thyme, crushed
4 large apples
16 medium kumquats
1 gallon water
1 onion
1 cup whipping cream
2 tablespoons lemon juice, freshly squeezed
4 truffles, freshly wrestled away from a pig
1 pint flammable substance like Vicks NyQuil, cherry-flavored

Hang the dead duck in your front window for a couple of days like they do in Europe.

Put on some relaxing mood music: "You Gotta Put Down the Duckie if You're Gonna Play the Saxophone," by the Muppets. I love that song.

Pluck the duck. Don't lick your fingers or you will feel down in the mouth. Gut the duck as you would a chicken.

Remove any obvious BBs. Sprinkle the inside of the duck with salt, pepper, and thyme. Cram in a couple of apples.

Bake the duck in the oven at 403 degrees for 1 1/2 hours. Turn the duck over and bake it awhile longer while basting. Take the duck out and discard the apples.

Fill a saucepan with 1/2 inches of water. (This is an actual quotation from a recipe book, but I have yet to see a saucepan you can fill with only 1/2 inch of water. You have to take these things with a grain of salt.)

Add a grain of salt.

Add the remaining apples and lemon juice. Cook them until tender. Eat them. You are probably quite hungry by now.

Put the truffles and kumquats in the blender on *frappé* for about ten minutes.

Order a pizza.

Siphon off a few quarts of duck fat. Pour some duck fat into a saucepan and add onion fragments. Sauté until your eyes water, and add mixture from the blender. Simmer for an hour or two adding a little NyQuil and the duck giblets. Strain into another pan and discard giblets.

Add whipped cream to the strained stuff, bring to a boil. Blend in the remaining NyQuil.

Pour the sauce mixture over the duck and set it on fire. Have the gallon of water nearby just in case.

Watch the duck burn while you polish off the last of your pizza. You could eat the duck but you used too much thyme.

Rocky Mountain Oysters

This is a favorite at quality, aristocratic restaurants like the Denver Macho Grill and Motorcycle Shop. Just take a bowl full of fresh Rocky Mountain Oysters to the kitchen and. . . uh. . .

take them and. . . uh. . . some people eat. . . uh. . . and they sometimes just skewer. . . and cook on the branding fire. . . uh. . . . I think I need to go lie down for an hour or two.

Classic Zucchini Cake

Finally someone gave me this ultimate zucchini recipe. It dates to when Prometheus decided to help Hercules get rid of some dead zucchini.

It is fast, easy, and delicious. You should try it. It combines something you would usually discard (excess zucchini) with ambrosia (chocolate).

This is a recipe that even mortals can make. I made it once with the help of young children.

The best way to start is to have your children get all the ingredients out on the table so you'll know you have everything.

DIRECTIONS

Turn your oven on to 375°.

Assuming you live at 7000 ft. elevation like I do.

Grease and flour a big cake pan.

Grease is the kitchen name for lard.

Cream together until you are tired of the gritty sound:

1/2 cup margarine

1/2 oil

Vegetable oil, not motor oil.

1 3/4 cup sugar

Add:

2 chicken eggs

"WHO BOILED ALL THE EGGS?"

2 tsp. vanilla

1/2 cup milk

Sifting together the following ingredients:

Let your kids help sift.

2 1/2 cups flour

1/2 tsp. baking powder

"Oh NO!" There were only two cups left. But I am trained in crisis management. I added 1/2 cup of Bisquick since it is mostly flour.

1 tsp. baking soda

Make sure you grab the correct yellow box. I have found that corn starch results in unusual cakes.

1/2 tsp. salt

2 tsp. cinnamon

I use 1 1/2 tsp. I don't want to prematurely embalm anyone.

1/2 tsp. cloves

Fresh from the Spice Islands off New Guinea.
"Daddy, Erik is sifting flour on me!"
"ERIK, GO SIT ON YOUR BED FOR FIVE MINUTES!"

3 Tbs. cocoa

This box of cocoa had been in the family for generations, and it looked like the chalk cliffs of Dover, only brown. Using a hammer and a screwdriver, I was able to chip out the required amount.

Add fresh, unincubated eggs to the wet ingredients.

Sweep up the flour that the kids have sifted.

Add the dry ingredients to the wet ingredients and stir.

Now is the time, if you are a serious batter eater, to get a tablespoon and chow down. If you wait until the next step, the batter will taste like chocolate mousse with lawn clippings in it.

Now, finely shred the zucchini.

(Until you have two cups of stuff that looks a cow tossed her cookies.)

Stir it into the batter.

Dump the batter into the cake pan, and sprinkle one cup chocolate chips on top.

I like those little midget chocolate chips.

Locate the chocolate chips.

Ask the kids if they know where they are.

"No". . ."No". . . . . . "No."

Try to remember what you did with the chocolate chips.

"Daddy, Erik won't give me any chocolate chips."

Adjust the recipe!

Instead of adding 1 cup, add 3/4 cup chocolate chips. You don't need all that chocolate anyway. Chocolate contains cocoa beans and calories and sugar and caffeine and insect parts.

Throw the pan into the oven.

Let it bake for 45 minutes.

I used two round cake pans, so I set the timer for 40 minutes. After about 20 minutes, I noticed strange combustion odors in the air, and I decided to check on the cake. I opened the oven and the bottom of the oven looked like Pompeii with two little round Vesuviuses dumping lava all over. Quickly I put a cookie sheet under the pans to catch some of the stuff. Maybe it was the Bisquick; perhaps I didn't eat enough batter; or maybe I should have used one of our industrial-sized pans.

Check for doneness.

You can tell it is done because you are tired and want to go to bed.

Let it cool for 15 minutes, and then try to dump it out of the pan.

> *Ha! It won't work. Those vanilla-flavored Styrofoam cakes you make from a cake mix will jump right out of a pan, but the zucchini cake is so moist it comes out of the pan in chunks, if at all. This is not all that bad, because with the cake lying upside down in heaps on a plate you can easily snitch a piece, and no one can tell you took any. This means that the cake will be gone in about five minutes.*

Baked Potatoes

Take two potatoes: One should be exactly 1 7/8 inches in diameter and one 2 inches in diameter.

Bacon bits
Sour cream
Salt
Pepper
Macadamia nuts
Cheddar cheese
Green onions
Sunflower seeds
Butter
Green chile

Bake the two potatoes until they are done. Slice open. Add toppings.

Invite friends to taste the two potatoes and see whether they can tell the difference.

Record your results and mail to the Department of Agriculture.

Soap

Making homemade soap gives you the opportunity to mix lard with hazardous chemicals in a large vat in your kitchen.

Soap occurs when fats are hydrolyzed with aqueous sodium hydroxide per the chemical reaction:

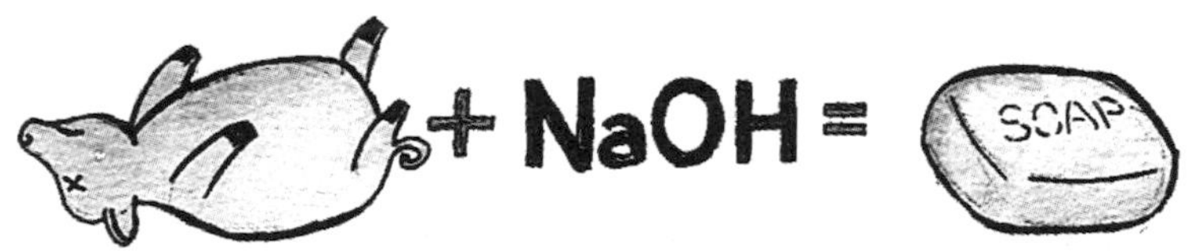

Why should you deliberately make soap in your kitchen instead of just buying it at the store?

1. You can save money, possibly several dollars a year after you replace the kitchen wallpaper.

2. Soap was invented so you have a use for lard other than eating it, which was OK for the pioneers who walked sixty miles a day, but not for the sedate yuppies of the Nineties.

Danger: Do not try this at home!

Recipe:
1/4 tsp. nutmeg
1 cardboard box
6.25 pounds pig fat
2 cups sifted all-purpose white flour
1 can (14 oz.) NaOH (commonly called Drano)
1 egg
1 enamel pan that you don't mind destroying
1/2 tsp. baking soda

1 two-gallon Pyrex beaker
1/2 cup sugar
2 gallons vinegar
1/2 cup sour milk
1 gigantic cheese cutter
1/4 tsp. salt
2 tablespoons ammonia (Warning: Ammonia is very dangerous.)
2 tablespoons borax powder
1/2 tsp. vanilla
Warning: Are you really sure you want to try this?

Line the cardboard box with a few paper grocery bags.
Sift flour, baking soda, and salt together.
Cook the pig fat in an enamel pan until it turns into lard with fried pig skins floating around on top.
Fork out the fried pig skins and drain on absorbent paper.
Put 2 tablespoons of the lard in a bowl, add sugar, and cream together until light and fluffy.
Add egg and beat well.
Stir in vanilla.
Add sour milk and sifted ingredients and blend together.
Roll dough out on a flowered surface.
Cut dough into ring shaped pieces.
Cook a batch of doughnuts in the hot lard.
Drain doughnuts on absorbent paper.
You forgot the nutmeg. Don't worry about it.

Cool the lard to 95 degrees F.

Note: Now is a good time to eat the doughnuts and pork skins and just forget the rest of the project.

Dump the lye into the glass beaker and slowly add cold water. Do this in a remote corner of your farm, away from all living things. The process is very exothermic which is a chemical term meaning "don't grab the beaker."

Warning: Don't spill any lye on your shoes.

Have tons of water and the vinegar ready for when you spill lye on your shoes. When the lye mixture stops boiling, volcano-like, and cools to 95 degrees, using twenty-foot tongs, slowly pour it into the hot lard, stirring constantly. Carefully dump the ammonia and borax powder into the pot and keep stirring. Stir the goop until it is the consistency of honey. Add the nutmeg if you feel like experimenting. Pour it into the lined cardboard box, cover with waxed paper and an old horse blanket or something else you never want to use again, and let it cool slowly for a few days. Cut the soap into blocks with the gigantic cheese cutter.

Use the soap to wash your hands after eating doughnuts or grate it with a Salad Shooter for laundry soap.

Makes about eight pounds of soap, eighteen doughnuts, and three ounces of pork skins.

Discussion questions:

- Did you have to read Macbeth in high school?
- Don't pork skins taste better with a little red chili?

INDEX

C

S

T

Order Form

Piñon Press
P. O. Box 4785
Los Alamos NM 87544

Please send me

____ Copies of Beginning Farming @ $9.00 each. ________

New Mexico residents add $.55 sales tax per book. ________

Add $1.50 shipping and handling per order ________

Total ________

Please ship to:

Name ______________________________

Street or PO Box ______________________________

City, State and Zip ______________________________

I am paying by Check Money Order Credit Card

Credit Card: VISA Mastercard Exp. Date____/__

Card # _ _ _ _ - _ _ _ _ - _ _ _ _ - _ _ _ _

For credit card orders, you may FAX it to 505-672-4098
E-Mail it on Prodigy to GYGF42B
E-Mail it on Compuserve to 75232,3671

Please allow two weeks for delivery.